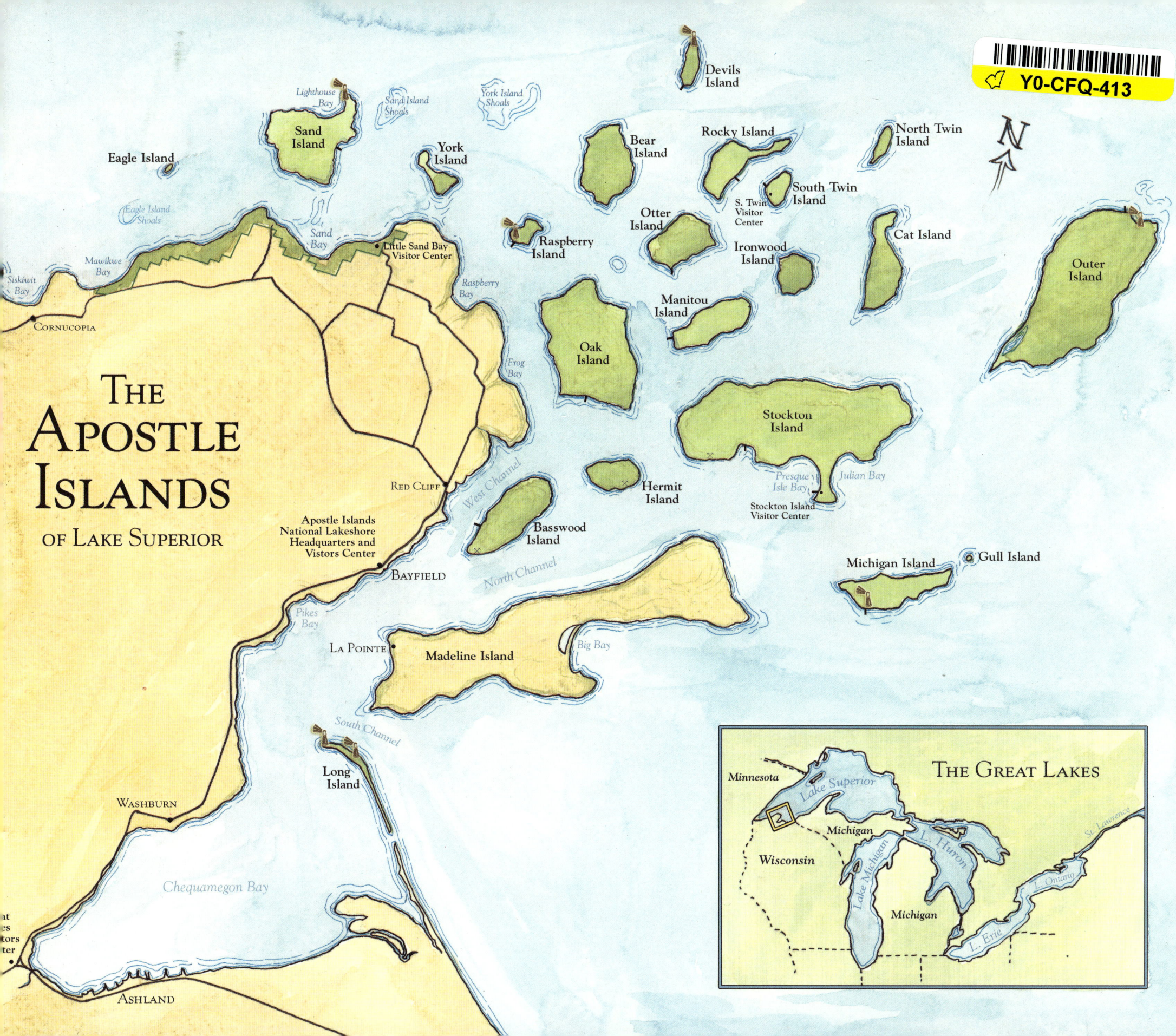

Jewels on the Water

LAKE SUPERIOR'S APOSTLE ISLANDS

TEXT BY JEFF RENNICKE
PHOTOGRAPHS BY LAYNE KENNEDY

Text © 2005 Jeff Rennicke
Photographs © Layne Kennedy (except historic photos and others as noted); website: www.laynekennedy.com

All rights reserved. No part of this book may be reproduced or transmitted in any form or by any means, electronic or mechanical, including photocopying, recording, placing on the internet, or by any information storage and retrieval system, without permission in writing from the publisher.

Published by
The Friends of the Apostle Islands National Lakeshore
PO Box 1574, Bayfield, WI 54814

For further park information see www.nps.gov/apis

Notes on uncaptioned photographs are printed on page 128.

Designed by Patricia Bickner Linder
Edited by Greg Linder and Patricia Bickner Linder
Printed in China

ISBN 0-9754331-0-5

Author's Acknowledgments
Knowledge of the islands comes one discovery at a time. Many people have helped me. I'd like to thank current and former National Park Service staff including Julie Van Stappen, Bob Mackreth, Susan Mackreth, David Snyder, Matt Welter, Neil Howk and Bob Krumenaker; guides Grant Herman and Gail Green who love these islands as I do and have shared some great trips; John Anderson for many trips and the pineapple, Bill Cronon for his insight and the front porch discussions; Julian Nelson, Marty Erickson, Martin Hanson and the Friends of the Apostles; Layne Kennedy for showing me the islands through new eyes; Ted Gephart for my first trip to the islands; and my family – Jill, Katelyn, and Hannah – and our friends Mike, Kathy, Shawn, and Heather Radtke for all the days we've left our footprints in island sands.
—Jeff Rennicke

Photographer's Acknowledgments
Producing any creative body of work requires help outside of those whose names are printed on the cover. To all those people who were in my images doing what they love, thank you. To those of you who appear on these pages but whom I never met, thanks, and I hope you get the chance to share in those captured moments. To Jeff and Jill Rennicke and their daughters Katelyn and Hannah, who put me up in their home for much of this project. I felt like I was home. What a wonderful gift. Thanks to John Anderson and Mary Boyle Anderson for their friendship and enthusiasm for taking part in any proposed lake experience and greatly assisting me with water transportation or as hiking partners, often at a moment's notice. Greg Alexander, a fellow artist whose passion for the outdoors made it easy to spend time with him on his boat exploring the islands. Bob Krumenaker, Park Superintendent, and his knowledgeable staff for input on important locations in the park, with help identifying species, and positive feedback for a project we're all thrilled to be doing. Designer Pat Linder for her skills and thoughtful input in keeping the book on target despite my own passionate approach to editing images. And to Martin Hanson, whose generous support and vision made this book a reality. His purpose in providing education and his support in keeping the Apostle Islands a recognized national treasure are immeasurable.
—Layne Kennedy

"... while in the distance like gems of living green, the far famed Apostle Islands."
—Bayfield Press, July 1877

To Hannah, my first mate on so many adventures among the islands.
—J.R.

To Dad,
The simple thrill of new discoveries along the paths I've taken motivate me to continue exploring. Knowing your life, taken too early, I wish I could've walked in your shoes for just a day.
—L.K.

Contents

Preface by William Bechtel, 6

Out of the Mist, 12

Dance of the Landscape, 20

Tracks, 30

The Echoes of History, 44

A Keeper's Tale, 60

Lifting Nets, 74

Among the Islands: A Journey in Postcards, 86

Preface

The Apostle Islands National Lakeshore is a rare treasure of natural beauty and fascinating history. It was not simply a "gift of nature." The National Lakeshore of today is a lucky outcome of the boom-and-bust history of the northland, followed by decades of unrelenting effort by people who recognized the recreational and ecological potential of the islands.

Among the first of these was President Calvin Coolidge, who in 1928 spent the summer fishing on the nearby Brule River at the urging of Senator Irvine Lenroot. At that time, the area was entering a deep economic decline as its resources of lumber, iron ore, fish, sandstone and productive farmland were practically tapped out. Business leaders who had expected Ashland to become "another Chicago" were suddenly thinking that tourism might offer hope for an economic future. Coolidge's yacht was followed from Ashland to Devils Island by a swarm of boats jammed with reporters and cameramen.

Coolidge spoke glowingly of the islands and the welcome he received. Congressman Hubert Peavey followed up with a bill to study the idea of a national park in the islands. Coolidge's successor, Herbert Hoover, signed the bill, but the ensuing federal review was extremely negative. Advocates did not give up; many proposals for a local, state or national park were offered, but went nowhere. The great depression and World War II then intervened.

In 1958, Wisconsin voters elected Gaylord Nelson as governor. By this time, efforts were underway at the federal level to expand recreational opportunities for Americans. Under President Eisenhower, the Outdoor Recreation Resources Commission (ORRC) report, championed by Laurence Rockefeller, recommended a

park in the islands. Gaylord subsequently developed the Outdoor Resources Acquisition Program (ORAP), a move that marked his emergence as an environmentalist. Urged on by associates Harold "Bud" Jordahl and Martin Hanson and his brother, the late Louis Hanson, Gaylord would devote much of his long political career to the Apostle Islands project.

In May, 1962, the Bad River Tribal Council called for study of a "National Shoreline-Recreation Area" in the Apostle Islands, region, including the Kakagon Sloughs, a unique part of the reservation. Governor Nelson endorsed this proposal and met with Interior Secretary Stewart Udall. A local Citizens Committee for an Apostle Islands National Lakeshore was formed. Bud Jordahl and the Hanson brothers went to many meetings and organizations locally and statewide to gain support. A key ally in mobilizing business and professional supporters was the late Dr. Bruce Culver Prentice of Ashland.

Once Gaylord became a US Senator in 1963, he made the Apostle Islands a priority. He had discussed a nationwide conservation tour with John Kennedy during the Wisconsin primary. Gaylord and his staff were invited to a White House luncheon with a staff person, Lee White, but White seemed unimpressed.

Then came one of those strange events that can change history. Washington reporters claimed they overheard Senator Nelson at a social event fuming at the White House over a badly handled political appointment. Gaylord was summoned to the White House, and asked me, as his chief of staff, to drive him there.

He emerged smiling, and explained: "A president can't be responsible for everything his staff does. Anyway, you are to meet with Jerry Bruno (a Kennedy advance man) and arrange a trip to the Apostle Islands, followed by a nationwide tour on the environment. And you are to draft a speech for the president on the Apostle Islands."

On September 24, 1963, Air Force One landed at Duluth. President Kennedy and the senator, joined by Interior Secretary Udall, Agriculture Secretary Freeman, Governor John Reynolds, and Martin Hanson, transferred to a fleet of helicopters and flew to the Apostle Islands, where 10,000 residents and 50 reporters and cameramen were assembling.

The pilot informed the president that a storm appeared to be developing over Ashland, and the crowd was larger than anticipated. We had planned a full tour of the islands, but given the situation, Martin suggested a short trip over the islands—just enough to give the reporters time to gather—and the president agreed. Flying lower over Basswood Island, several sailboats on the lake caught Kennedy's attention. Martin commented that the Apostles are excellent for sailing, pointing out that the lee sides of the islands offer safety from Lake Superior storms. The president, himself a sailor, smiled broadly.

In his speech at Ashland, Kennedy praised Lake Superior—"this great inland sea"—and said every day that was not spent preserving these precious resources was "a day wasted." It was a stunning public, political and governmental triumph, seemingly assuring quick approval of a long-held dream.

Tragically, two months later President Kennedy was dead.

Kennedy had stopped short of endorsing Gaylord's bill, and it would undergo eight drafts before finally passing. Land issues were extremely sensitive. A new Republican state administration, including some conservation officials who had differences with Gaylord, expressed doubts. Questions were raised as to how state-owned islands would fit into a national park. Traditional budget cutters fretted about acquisition and development costs. Private landowners hired lawyers to fight the plan. Some people complained that the Federal government already owned too much of northern Wisconsin. Local sportsmen feared they would lose favorite hunting and fishing spots.

Senator Nelson meanwhile made a new bid for presidential support—from Lyndon Johnson. Gaylord and his staff met with Joseph Califano, the president's top political advisor, and urged that the Apostle Islands bill be included in the president's budget. Califano showed real interest. Nelson got a follow-up invitation to the Johnson ranch in Texas, but it was never revealed whether they discussed the number one question.

In early 1967, the senator's office received a phone call: "It's in the budget!" Suddenly other calls poured in from federal agencies and congressional offices. People in Washington wanted to know all about Wisconsin's Apostle Islands.

A Senate public hearing was held in Ashland in June 1967. At the hearing, Governor Warren Knowles and his conservation agencies announced their support, and pledged state-owned islands to the federal park. The Senate passed the bill on August 21, 1967, but the battle dragged on in the House of Representatives. In 1969 Republican Richard Nixon replaced Democrat Lyndon Johnson, raising new uncertainty.

House negotiators removed much of the proposed mainland property from the park, including all Indian lands, at the request of the Indians. The National Park Service came close to ruling that the project was no longer worthy of federal park recognition. Eventually, the problems were resolved, the Senate accepted the House amendments, and President Nixon signed the bill on September 26, 1970.

The park was expanded in 1986 when Congressman David Obey won approval of a bill to add Long Island to the National Lakeshore, and President Ronald Reagan signed it. The island, a long spit of sand which extends into Chequamegon Bay and forms the Ashland harbor, had been found to be a nesting site for the endangered piping plover. Protection became imperative.

Wisconsin's US Senator Russell Feingold requested a study on possible wilderness areas within the Apostle Islands National Lakeshore, resulting in a National Park Service proposal for wilderness status. The Friends of the Apostle Islands approved of the wilderness designations along with the political parties, both Democrat and Republican, of Ashland and Bayfield Counties.

Congressman Obey attached the wilderness bill to an appropriations bill which President George W. Bush signed into law in 2004.

With over 40 years of congressional deliberation, local controversy, countless hours of negotiation, and the cooperation of presidents Coolidge, Hoover, Kennedy, Johnson, Nixon, Reagan and Bush, the Apostle Islands National Lakeshore, with the new Gaylord A. Nelson Wilderness Area, finally became the public treasure that it is today.

No, it wasn't just a gift from nature.

—*William R. Bechtel*
February 2005

Debarking the helicopter at Ashland in 1963, from left to right: Governor John Reynolds, Interior Secretary Stewart Udall, President John F. Kennedy, Secretary of Agriculture Orville Freeman, Martin Hanson, and Senator Gaylord Nelson.
Opposite: President Coolidge sizing up lunch at Devils Island.

Out of the Mist

Guide Grant Herman cups his hands around his mouth and bellows into the fog: "WhoooooWHOOP!" Our pod of five kayaks drifts quietly as our ears strain for the ricochet of his voice off the cliffs, any hint that were are nearing an island.

Nothing; just the soft *shhhhhh* of mist against the hood of my raincoat. Somewhere just ahead, we hope, lie the Apostle Islands. There should be blonde sand beaches and blueberries, cliffs brushed with the white tips of waves, and pines swaying in the breeze. There should be sailboats cupped to the wind, lighthouses blinking, and powerboats bobbing on their bowlines. But for now there is only a curtain of gray. The islands, it seems, have vanished.

"Let's paddle a few more minutes on this heading and check again," Grant says, and with a stroke of his paddle disappears into the swirling fog. The rest of us point our kayaks toward the crease in the clouds and follow, paddling deeper into the mist.

It is fitting to see—or not to see—the Apostles this way. For centuries, this constellation of islands spangling the waters of Lake Superior off Wisconsin's northern shore has seemed as much rumor as reality. Early maps show the islands drifting in and out of existence like phantoms, changing shape and size and number with every re-drawing. Twelve, one map would say. Two. Thirteen. Twenty-eight, insisted others.

Some of the confusion rests with outdated mapping techniques, some with the vagaries of memory. But Lake Superior itself may be at least partly to blame. Over 300 miles long and 160 miles wide, Superior is by surface area the largest freshwater lake on the planet. On such an expanse, numbering islands can be as difficult as counting stars. Islands seem to gather and vanish like apparitions in the mist, to float above the water in certain light; to drift with the wind in fog.

If that weren't enough, the names of the islands, too, have changed like autumn leaves. To the Ojibwe they were *Wigobic Miniss* (now called Basswood Island), *Mako Miniss* (now Bear Island), *Marchemanitou* (now Devils Island), *Nabikwana*

(now Eagle Island), and so forth. The French voyageurs added their accent as well: Stockton Island was *Presque Isle* and Basswood Island *Isle Michele*. In 1874 explorer Henry Schoolcraft assigned each the name of a state. South Twin was *Georgia*, Rocky Island became *Mississippi* and so on. Hermit Island has been called *Askew* and *Wilson's*. North Twin has been *Brownstone* and *Cat*, while Cat Island has been called everything from *Texas* to *Hemlock* to *Shoe*.

Collectively they have worn many names as well. They were the *Islands of Chagaouimigong*, a French version of the Ojibwe name, the *Federation Islands* to Schoolcraft. It was the Jesuit priests who first called them the Apostles, a name in common use by 1744 that could have sprung from a mistaken count of 12.

By any name these islands capture the heart and the imagination, as well as the spirit. When you can see them, that is.

Opposite: Fog off Stockton Island obliterates the vastness of Lake Superior beyond Julian Bay.
Inset: Dew temporarily reveals the shape of a spider's elaborate web —one reward of rising early near an island bog.
Above: Kayakers ply their way across calm, fog-shrouded water. The closed deck of a kayak offers a small safeguard against Lake Superior's changeable conditions.

This etching of a very busy Chequamegon Bay appeared in *Frank Leslie's Illustrated Newspaper* in 1887. Ashland is in the foreground, Washburn just across the Bay, and Bayfield near the point.

"There!" Grant Herman hollers as spires of spruce poke their way through the fog just ahead. Slowly, an island materializes before our eyes—tall sandstone cliffs pockmarked by the waves, a dozen herring gulls as white as dabs of paint perched on a ledge. A cove and a small beach, right where the maps say they should be.

Today those maps have settled on 22 islands in the Apostles chain. Twenty-one of them (all except Madeline) are now a part of the Apostle Islands National Lakeshore. Designated in 1970 and expanded in 1986, the Lakeshore throws the loop of its boundaries around 450 square miles of lake and islands as well as a 12-mile stretch of the mainland shore. There is Stockton Island where the sand "sings" under your bare feet and sandhill cranes bugle from the bogs. There is Devils Island with its red-eyed lighthouse and Gull where the summer sky is stirred by thousands of wings. There are Oak and Outer, Manitou and Bear, Cat Island, York Island, Michigan, and more.

To a kayaker moving silently along on a day when the fog blurs the edges, or a sailor crossing a reach at sunrise, these islands can seem as wild and remote as the last stars in the morning sky. There are docks on some of them, strips of boardwalks in places, a few trail signs, but there is not a single maintained road on any of the islands within the Apostle Islands National Lakeshore. Some have no developed campgrounds or even trails. There are no bus tours or lodges. Away from the docks and the campgrounds you are more likely to find the heart-shaped tracks of deer than human footprints, and a silence broken only by the verse of the surf.

In places these islands can seem as untouched and untouchable as the highest mountain top. But look closely. The cribbing of an old dock appears beneath your kayak. Hiking a trail, you find the bricks of a tumbled chimney strewn in the brush or the long, rusted teeth of an old hayrick silent in the grass. There amidst an open field, a grove of apple trees in what was once a family orchard.

There is a long human history woven into the fabric of these islands. That history has sometimes left its mark carved into the island's bedrock and

14

sometimes left nothing more than a few graying planks weathering namelessly along a shore. But it is a history just the same. Voyageurs came here dreaming of fortunes in fur. Lumbermen dreamt of pine. Boat captains have for centuries run for a lee among the islands to wait out a storm while hermits stayed to weather different, more personal storms. Farmers, fishermen, lighthouse keepers, presidents, and paupers found their way to the islands, charmed by the lull of the lake and drawn by whatever dreams put a glint in their eyes.

Today, people come to the Apostles for other reasons. They come to hike a trail beneath a canopy of leaves where the rustle in the shadows might mean "bear," and to climb a lighthouse to peer into history. They come to sail and to dive and to fish and to swing their legs over the edge of a dock and watch the clouds drift by like the hours. They come to be among the islands.

Islands are a place apart. They are not of the mainland, exactly, but not completely of the lake either. They are other worlds set apart by the deep blue space of the lake. Something falls away from you as the boat slips its lines and clears the dock—a heaviness of spirit. And something alights in you as well—a sense of adventure and

Top: An early postcard depicted an Ojibwe mother and girls going to gather blueberries.
Left: Recreational boating enjoys a long history in the Apostles.

A camper looks out from the dock at Sand Island, as the morning sun begins to burn off the fog to slowly reveal the horizon. Opposite: A kayaker camping on Basswood Island retrieves fresh water from Lake Superior.

anticipation, and the realization that you are going someplace special. Up ahead on the horizon lies a place where human dreams and nature's will mix like wind and waves—a place of silence and foghorns, time and timelessness. Just ahead lies an island.

By the time our kayaks round the point, the fog is lifting. Other islands begin to appear out of the mist, sparkling in the rain-washed light. It happens slowly. Tatters of fog will cling to the trees like gray-white ribbons for hours, but that seems fitting, too. These islands reveal themselves slowly. No matter how you come here—by sail or paddle, powerboat or on the excursion boat—the Apostles cannot be taken in all at once or captured as easily as a postcard sunset. They are too much for that. There are stories among these islands, but they come slowly, one lifting fog, one wave, one island, one story at a time.

Above: Sportfishing around the islands holds the promise of sizeable lake trout such as this.
Opposite: Lake Superior's wardrobe contains a multitude of hues, as seen here from the Lakeshore Trail.

The Dance of the Landscape

Any story of the Apostle Islands must begin with this: the sound of water on rock. The geology of the islands has been a dance of water and rock from the very beginning. The Orienta, Devils Island, and Chequamegon sandstones, the three types of stone that form the bedrock of the Apostles (except for Long Island, which is underlain by sand) were laid down by the sweeps and swirls of ancient rivers and lakes, beginning nearly a billion years ago. The fingerprints of those currents and waves are still visible in the "ripple rocks" found along the shore. These sandstones, brought in by northeastern-trending rivers and streams, were buried by younger rocks now worn away by time and water. But the real sculptor of the islands was ice.

Time and again in the last 2.5 million years, the cold, blunt chisel of glaciers has carved away at this land. The last major ice flow, some 12,000 years ago, snaked its way down from the northeast, entombing the islands in a thousand-foot-thick layer of grinding and carving ice. Lower islands—Cat, Rocky, South Twin, Sand, and others—were quickly covered, the claws of the ice leaving deep grooves known as "glacial striae" that are still visible on Stockton Island and other places today. Higher islands, like Oak and Bear, may at first have split the lobes of the advancing ice like boulders in a stream, but they too would eventually be overrun, leaving only wind, ice, and the slow tick of time.

Then the ice began to melt. Around 11,500 years ago, a shift in temperatures halted the glaciers' advance, melting the ice and unleashing an almost unfathomable torrent of meltwater to further chip away at the islands, deepening the channels between them and sculpting their edges. Great boulders, swirled by the currents, hollowed out "potholes" visible in the rocks of Lighthouse Bay on Sand Island. Huge blankets of debris, rocks, and gravel settled on the islands as the ice melted, or were piled up by the torrential flows, leaving the glacial bluffs seen on Michigan, Raspberry, Oak, and other islands today. The levels of ancient Lake Superior rose and fell as great lobes of ice melted, grew, and began to melt again.

Slowly, the lake levels receded, uncovering the islands one by one. Oak Island, the highest with an elevation of 1,081 feet, was the first, then Bear, Stockton, and others. By 10,500 years ago, all of the Apostles poked out of the lake, appearing as if by magic, as the blue cloth of the water was slowly drawn back.

But the islands that dotted the lake of 10,000 years ago would hardly be recognizable to sailors and paddlers today. Water, storms, ice, and wind have altered the faces of the islands, shaping and reshaping them like the crystals of a kaleidoscope. Lake levels rose, splitting one island at a low point and creating two. Great fingers of sand deposited by storms formed "tombolos" that united two islands into one.

York Island may once have been two separate islands. Presque Isle Point was cut off from the rest of Stockton Island until between 2,500 and 5,000 years ago. Gull Island was once a part of Michigan Island. What we now call Long Island is not really an island at all, but a long, sandy peninsula cut off from the mainland only during times of high storm waves.

Sometimes whole islands simply vanish. As recently as 1890, an island known as Little Steamboat poked above the water just south of where Eagle Island stands today, only to be erased from the lake and from maps by the erosive lashing waves of a particularly storm-tossed winter.

And the dance continues. Geology never stops. Every wave, each thrust of sand-blasting wind or shove of the ice, changes things slightly, carves a sea cave more deeply, etches out a crack that will become an arch or topple one. In 1975, the arch

known as Lookout Point on Hermit Island collapsed. Honeymoon Rock on the far end of Basswood Island has changed significantly from the postcard views of the early 1900s. Twenty foot spires of rock called "sea stacks" in Justice Bay on Sand

Opposite: Grasses gain a foothold on deposited sand, marking a transition in the landscape.
Inset: Patterns decorate the impressionable surface of sandstone.
Above: Thin layers of sandstone are visible where the waves have carved out caves and pillars.

Island have vanished in a single winter.

Stand today at a lookout on the Lakeshore Trail atop the Mawikwe caves and the rock beneath your boots seems solid. It is comforting, but it is an illusion. We live our lives on too short a timescale to see anything more than a snapshot of these islands. Still, if we could glimpse them through different eyes, seeing them in geologic time, streaks of glacial ice would snap back and forth like bolts of lightning, and arches would open and close as quickly as blinking eyes. After such a view, we would never see a cliff or wave in quite the same way again. What seems solid today will be brushed away in time. The breaking of every wave is a lesson in what remains; each drop of melting ice is another tick of the clock. It is all a part of the dance of the landscape.

Left: The Stockton Island tombolo connects Presque Isle Point to the rest of the island. The powerful waves produced by Superior's storms pushed the exposed sand into a series of beach ridges, where vegetation began to grow on the higher sand, stabilizing it. Lagoons later formed as the low areas between the ridges filled with water.
Opposite: On Stockton Island's eastern side, large rocks have broken away from the shore, part of the process that continues to change the appearance of the islands.

Chiseled by ice and smoothed by the slow erosion of water, the rocks of Lake Superior bear gifts of nature's artistry, such as this crescent moon on Devils Island. Opposite: A perfect outpost for nesting cliff swallows, Balancing Rock stands precariously off the shore of Stockton Island.

Where the Waves Come to Play

On the far western end of the Apostle Islands National Lakeshore, just beyond the last footprints in the sands of Meyers Beach, a row of cliffs rises burnt orange against the blue water. This is where the waves come to play.

Slapped by the waves and chiseled by the ice, the cliffs of Mawikwe Bay (formerly Squaw Bay) are proof of the artistry of rock and water.

The rock is Devils Island sandstone, part of the billion year-old Bayfield Group. Of the three types of sandstone among the Apostles, the Orienta is the oldest, the Chequamegon is most quarried for building stone and the Devils Island sandstone is the most artistic. Laid down in shallow lakes and ponds, it is fine-grained, thinly bedded rock, no match for the power of waves, ice and time.

When the lake is open the cliffs, unprotected by outlying islands, are pummeled by storm waves gouging holes known as "reentrants" at the water line. As these reentrants deepen, weaker layers above collapse, making the caves still deeper. Reentrants sometimes join, creating intricate and elaborate mazes of caverns, isolating spires and arches. It is a process that never stops. In 1987 a formation known as Elephant Rock, often depicted in local postcards, collapsed in rubble changing the face of the cliffs.

Pounding waves and prying ice constantly reshape exposed rock faces, carving out caves, breaking away rock, and smoothing its surfaces.

Winter adds its touches, too. Ice floes jam against the cliffs, acting like a rasp, filing away at the sandstone walls. More intricate touches are added by the constant thaw and freeze cycle of winter. Water seeps into the cracks then freezes, expanding as it does, prying apart the thin layers and cracking the rock.

The result is a gallery of cliffs a mile long and up to 100 feet high—sculpted, scoured, chiseled, and cracked into an art form. There are cliff walls with holes in the rock where the wind whistles

Left: This old postcard demonstrates the changing nature of the islands. It depicts "Grand Arch" on Sand Island, a stone edifice that no longer exists.

through like a flute player, and arches the size of great halls. There are sea stacks like exclamation points of rock and natural bridges that span the waves.

The same process has carved similar caves at other places in the park—the northern tip of Devils Island and Swallow Point on Sand Island—but the Mawikwe caves are the most accessible and the most popular with visitors. By summer the caves draw sea kayakers who paddle the maze of passageways and cracks, moving deep into the shadows where the rock is lit by emerald green light shining up through the water. Cool temperatures and moist conditions in the caves create a kind of microclimate for uncommon mosses and sedges, some found nowhere else in the state.

In winter, the caves glitter with ice—cliff faces strung with stalactites of ice, frozen waterfalls dyed by minerals in the rocks to red and green, ice chandeliers, frozen lightning bolts clinging to the rock. When ice conditions are right, hikers and skiers move from room to room in a palace of ice. They come clumsily at first, each step a clattering of ice crystals, exclaiming at the frozen fireworks. But the sight stills them somehow. Entering a cave, they fall silent, whispering, afraid to touch anything or even breathe for fear that they might disturb the delicate latticework of the ice.

Beneath the silence, however, there are other sounds—the treble notes of water dripping, the slow drumming of waves restless beneath the ice. The lake is always moving. Water is always dripping, delivering another chip with the chisel, another brushstroke in the never-ending artwork of time.

At Mawikwe Bay, the caves become marvels of ice in winter. When conditions are right, visitors can ski or hike across the frozen lake to admire the stalactites, frozen waterfalls, and sculptural formations in and around the caves.

27

Tracks

There is more to these islands than rock and water. On a cool summer morning, still wrapped in quiet darkness, I slip out from my tent at Presque Isle campground on Stockton Island to feel my way slowly along the Tombolo Trail. Through the latticework of pines, I hike to where the trees fall away and the sky opens with stars. There I find a place to sit and wait.

At first there is little sound—the slow *shush* of waves on Julian Bay, a whisper of wind. But as light seeps into the darkness, sounds begin to grow—slivers of bird calls, the low chatter of ducks. A chorus of frogs is touched off by the growing light and soon the bugling of sandhill cranes. By the time the first rays of sun brush the trees, the soundscape is a full-throated roar. Calls and bellows, chirps and whistles rise like mist. It is morning in the bog.

Prior to the coming of axes and plows, the Apostles were draped 90 percent by mixed coniferous and hardwood forest of white pine, hemlock, sugar maple and birch. Those species are still here, in smaller numbers, but logging, farming, fires, and nature's resilience have created on the islands an intricate and complex web of life, a mix of nature's will and human endeavors.

There are sandscapes where the grasses draw delicate circles in the sand and shorebirds dance with the waves, and there are patches of old growth with silence as deep as the moss. There are young hardwood forests glowing orange in autumn, and bogs dotted with high-stepping herons, pitcher plants and orchids with names like "Rose Pogonia" and "dragon's mouth."

The numbers are impressive: over 800 species of plants. Some, like bird's-eye primrose and butterwort on Devils Island are found nowhere else in Wisconsin. Thirty-five mammal species, 150 kinds of resident breeding birds and as many as 200 bird species that migrate through. There are four species of snakes (eastern garter, northern red-bellied, northern ring-necked, and smooth green snake); two species of turtles (western painted and the eastern snapping); and at least 310 species of lichen.

Life thrums in these islands. And it consists of more than a list of numbers and species. It is the rich smells, the sounds of life rising off a morning bog, a flutter of wings in the dark. It's a set of tracks, just now visible in the growing light—bear tracks making for the beach.

Bears have been documented on many of the islands, including Basswood, Long, Sand, Raspberry, Manitou, Rocky, Hermit, Devils, and even Outer Island. Yet no place in the Lakeshore is as webbed with bear tracks as Stockton. To see a wild bear feeding in the blueberries or a sow and its cubs crossing a beach in a slant of evening light is to look nature straight in the eye. It is a sight that draws the eye like lightning, searing itself deep into the memory. Even a line of tracks can be a gift, a reminder of what a privilege it is to walk the same horizons as a creature as powerful and wild as a bear.

Bear tracks were once a rare sight in these islands. The original old-growth forests offered little habitat. But openings created by lumbering, fire, and agriculture drew the bears across the waters. Martin Kane, an "itinerant island-dweller, fisherman, sugar-boiler and moonshine distiller" who lived on Oak in the 1930s and 40s, kept a pair of bear hounds, named "Rex" and "Schnapps," and claimed to have taken many bears. On Stockton Julian Nelson, who fished here from 1919 to 1947, and whose name still graces

Opposite, inset: A grove of paper birch stands along the Lakeshore Trail on the mainland.
Left: False rue anemone, a wildflower, emerges from a long winter on Devils Island.
Right: Tracks testify to the meandering of a black bear across the sands of Julian Bay on Stockton Island.

Above: Bird and animal tracks litter the dunes at Julian Bay on Stockton Island, amid pines shaped by the buffeting of storms.

the beautiful beach on the island's northeastern side, cannot recall seeing a single bear. In 1984, only three bears were confirmed on the island. That number grew to 12 by 1986; topped 25 in 1991; and reached 31 in 1994. A recent National Park Service study confirmed 26 adult and yearling bears on Stockton. With cubs, that number that could top 40 animals in spring, giving the island a density of 2.1 bears per square mile—double that of the mainland and one of the greatest concentrations of black bears anywhere in North America.

Such a high density speaks both to the quality of the habitat and the size of Stockton Island, the largest in the Apostle Islands National Lakeshore. Seeing a bear is still rare but on Stockton Island they prowl the circle of seasons, scouring the marshes for the tender greens of spring, gorging on blueberries in high summer, searching for acorns and insects in fall, and curling like dark seeds against the cold in winter dens beneath the roots of upturned trees.

Yet even good habitat has its limits. Bears on Stockton are smaller—yearlings up to 40 pounds lighter than their peers on the mainland. Home ranges are smaller and often overlap. Female island bears breed later and have smaller litter sizes. And it can be a tough place for young bears. The cub survival rate is lower than on the mainland.

And then there are the people. Stockton, with its marina, campground, fireside ranger talks, and picturesque beaches, is the most visited island in the Apostle Islands National Lakeshore. Here, bear tracks mix with human footprints. While there has never been a single incident of a bear injuring a human in the Apostle Islands National Lakeshore, things have not always been completely peaceful.

The most famous encounter involved a three-year-old male nicknamed "MacArthur" for its propensity to return again and again to Stockton Island. Trapped in 1988 at Trout Point, the bear was given a red radio collar by researchers, making it easy to recognize when it tore into a tent to lick clean a frying pan in the campground, plundered garbage cans at the ranger's quarters and approached a crowd gathered at the fire ring for a ranger talk.

The final straw came on July 31, 1988. That night a trio of boats rocked softly at the Presque Isle dock: the *Atlantis*, the *Arrowhead*, and the *Sugar n' Spice*. Sometime after midnight, lured by the scent of grilled food, the bear padded down the dock and brazenly boarded each boat in turn, ripping a hatch cover aboard the *Atlantis* before it was driven off by a barking dog.

A bear accustomed to human food is like a lit fuse, or as park literature puts it, "a fed bear is often a dead bear." Something had to be done. Park rangers captured the bear in a culvert trap, relocating it on August 16 to the Chequamegon National Forest 20 miles south of Bayfield. But the story doesn't end there. Outfitted with a radio transmitter, the bear was followed as it worked its way back to the shore near Cornucopia and then to the tip of the Bayfield Peninsula. For a time the signal was lost. On September 18, it was picked up again, back on Stockton Island. Over the next summer the bear was spotted several times—once swimming to Oak and another time swimming to the mainland before again heading for the familiar shores of its home island.

Finally, in the fall of 1989, the radio transmitter stopped working. The collar fell off and "MacArthur," named for the famous general who once said "I shall return!" caused no more trouble and quietly faded into island history.

Not every bear has been so lucky. In 2003 another famous Stockton Island bear, this one nicknamed "Skar" for a large wound on its flank, was killed by rangers at Quarry Bay after repeatedly threatening campers and causing property damage. That same year, seven other bears had to be removed from Oak Island.

Still, for every story such as these there have been thousands of peaceful sightings, most consisting of quick glimpses of fur in the shadows. Bear tracks fringe the islands with a kind of wildness not felt in many places. The horizons seem wider, the shadows deeper, the islands wilder because there are bears. With continuing public education on how to live respectfully in bear country, and with the forbearance of bears, perhaps the Apostles will always remain a place where bear tracks and human footprints can safely mix.

Bear tracks are not the only tracks to etch the

Above: Deer numbers soared in the wake of heavy logging. In the 1950s, intensive hunting, such as this successful hunt on Rocky Island, sought to arrest the population boom in the Apostle Islands. Left: On islands where whitetails are abundant, their appetites pose a threat to the establishment, and the survival, of some plant species.

deer. Another in 1938 found only "a few deer tracks." A 1946 aerial search found them on nine islands. Yet by the mid-1950s, Basswood, Hermit, and Manitou were beginning to show signs of overpopulation. At the same time, Rocky Island was experiencing what one biologist called "the fastest buildup of a deer population and the fastest degeneration of habitat" he had ever seen.

Intensive hunts were organized. Local outfitters offered guided hunts. In 1954 over 400 deer were harvested off the Apostles—275 from Rocky and Stockton alone. Such a rapid build up of the deer population meant the some islands were stripped of some plant species, literally eaten out of house and home. Unchecked deer populations can cause a drastic decline in plants such as the endangered Canada yew, a favorite food of whitetails. On islands where few if any deer have been documented, Canada yew thrives. On those islands threaded with deer tracks, it has nearly vanished.

Such small, isolated islands could not support high numbers of deer for long. Hunting and the harsh winters of the 1960s took their toll, as did a regrowth of the dense forests after logging was halted. By the 1970s so few were seen that hunting records for individual islands were no longer kept. By the 1980s deer were known to inhabit only a very few of the Apostles. Today, deer populations may be found on Oak, Basswood, and Sand Islands, as well as the mainland. Transient animals frequent Long, Stockton, and several other islands.

If bird flight left trails in the air then the skies

Above: Nesting herring gulls, top, and a herring gull chick.
Opposite page: A nesting colony of double-crested cormorants on Eagle Island. This large black bird, whose diet consists mainly of fish, is common on Lake Superior.

islands. The prints of snowshoe hare punctuate the snow of nearly every island. Beaver tails slap the waters on Sand and Michigan Islands. There are muskrat tracks in the mud of the Sand River and otter on many of the islands including Devils, Michigan, Outer, Sand, and Stockton. Foxes visit many of the islands, most often in winter, and ice fishermen report seeing coyotes crossing to the islands on the ice.

The white-tailed deer, like the bear, came late to the Apostles, the way cleared for them as the thick old forests fell to the axe creating the openings they prefer. A survey of seven islands in 1919 found no

34

⚓ 35

Right: National emblem and conservation success story, the bald eagle was nearly wiped out thirty years ago. In 1981 there were no active nests in the Apostle Islands; in 2004, 13 breeding nests were counted, and 16 eagles fledged. Far right: Several of the islands host great blue heron rookeries.

Above: A rotting tree trunk provides a feast for insects and the insects provide a feast for birds such as woodpeckers. The cavities may in turn become home to cavity-nesting birds.
Right: Canada geese glide across a lagoon on Stockton Island. The species normally nests to the north in Canada, but may occasionally breed in the northern Great Lakes area.

above the islands would be covered with tracks, too. A hundred and fifty species of birds nest among the Apostles— redstarts and red-eyed vireos, ovenbirds, sandpipers, and crows. Birds frame nearly every island experience. Loons laugh in the bays, merlins slice the air like feathered lightning, great horned owls moan to a moon rising through the dark branches. Windbound once on York Island, I watched a trio of ravens playing in the wind, flying straight into the maw of the gale, rowing the black oars of their wings out over the lake until it seemed the next gust would rip them feather from bone, then tilting their wings to ricochet back to the safety of the trees.

Eighty percent of all the herring gulls that breed along Wisconsin's Lake Superior shore nest on Gull and Eagle Islands, the two smallest islands in the Lakeshore. Although Gull is just three acres, it can be home to over a thousand nests of herring gulls and cormorants. Eagle, at 26 acres, hosts up to 500 more as well as the only great blue heron rookery in the islands. The air vibrates with wings on a summer day. It is such vital nesting habitat that both islands are closed to public visitation during the nesting season.

The islands probably once were habitat for the passenger pigeon. A fur trader in July of 1804 bragged of killing 24 of the now-extinct birds on the mainland just south of Long Island. But the islands have provided habitat vital to the recovery of at least two other endangered species. The piping plover, a bird whose pale plumage and whirling wings make it resemble the wind-blown sand on which it lives, has returned to nesting sites on the beaches of Long Island after a 15-year absence. The bird is federally listed as endangered, and Long Island hosts the only active nest in Wisconsin. Long Island and the Michigan sandspit were designated as critical habitat for the piping plover by the U.S. Fish and Wildlife Service in 2001. Bald eagles, gone from the islands and much of the country by the 1970s due to pesticide contamination, nest again on Michigan, Rocky, Sand, York, Outer Island, and others.

In addition to important nesting habitat, the islands are vital for migratory birds. The only dry land resting points for flocks crossing western Lake Superior, the islands act as stepping stones. Huge numbers of birds stream across the Apostles, moving north in spring and south in fall, their flights tying these islands in with places as far away as the Arctic and Central America, binding them with ribbons of wings. Bird surveys on Outer Island in spring have counted as many as 800 hawks, mostly broad-wings, spiraling in the air at once. To

Above: Red-breasted merganser, normally a coastal bird, may be seen swimming and diving in the waters around the Apostle Islands. Insets, from top: The future of the endangered piping plover (shown here in a photo taken outside the park) may depend upon its protection in the Apostle Islands National Lakeshore; Wilson's snipe (center) and the spotted sandpiper (this one photographed at the mouth of Whittlesey Creek in the Chequamegon Bay) nest in the park.

Below: Beaver dams such as this one on Outer Island alter the landscape profoundly, adding habitat that will support more diversity.

songbirds, Outer Island is a touchstone of fall migration, the air above the sandspit rustling with wings. During an exceptional migration year, more than 140,000 birds of 107 species were counted there—as many as 28,000 an hour, resting, feeding, waiting for just the right winds to carry them to the mainland. A more typical migration season may see 50,000 birds with an average of 600 per hour.

As writer Michael Van Stappen has noted, it is "a wild circus" of birds. "Standing on that sandspit with birds streaming by in farewell flight to the mainland and places far beyond," wrote Van Stappen in his book *Northern Passage*, "the overwhelming urge is not to ponder or wonder, not to linger or go home. It is autumn, and in your heart the singular, deeply felt sense is to follow."

Life on an island always presents special risks. Limited space, changing conditions, competition and other factors make islands an ecological roll of the dice for wildlife and plants. It is a game that not all species win. Moose have been documented in the Chequamegon Bay area, the remains of a young bull discovered as recently as 1995 on Stockton Island. Still, moose have never established themselves here as they have on Isle Royale. Red squirrels chatter on the islands, but the Eastern gray squirrel does not. No striped skunks, woodchucks, or porcupines have been documented on the islands within the Lakeshore. Raccoons are found on the mainland and even on Madeline Island, but have not yet made their way to the other islands.

Even a little help from humans is not always enough. Pine marten were twice released on Stockton, once in 1953 and again in 1956, but it is unlikely they thrive there today. In 1949 the Wisconsin Conservation Department hatched a plan to establish a game bird hunting reserve on Outer Island, and released 13 black grouse and 33 Swedish Uhr hens (capercaillie) imported from Scandinavia. It didn't last long. The black grouse whirled their way back over the lake the moment the cages were opened. One Uhr hen survived the winter but was never seen again.

Every plant, every animal, every insect and bird that does survive on the islands today is the living

Above: the pitcher plant's rarely seen blossom.
Left: hairs line the inside of the pitcher plant's hood. The pitcher plant is carnivorous—an adaptation to the bog's nitrogen-poor soils. Insects entering the tube-shaped leaf are prevented by the hairs from climbing out. Liquid at the base of the tube dissolves the prey.
Right: In northern bogs the diminutive pitcher plant is easy to miss, nearly hidden among lush vegetation.

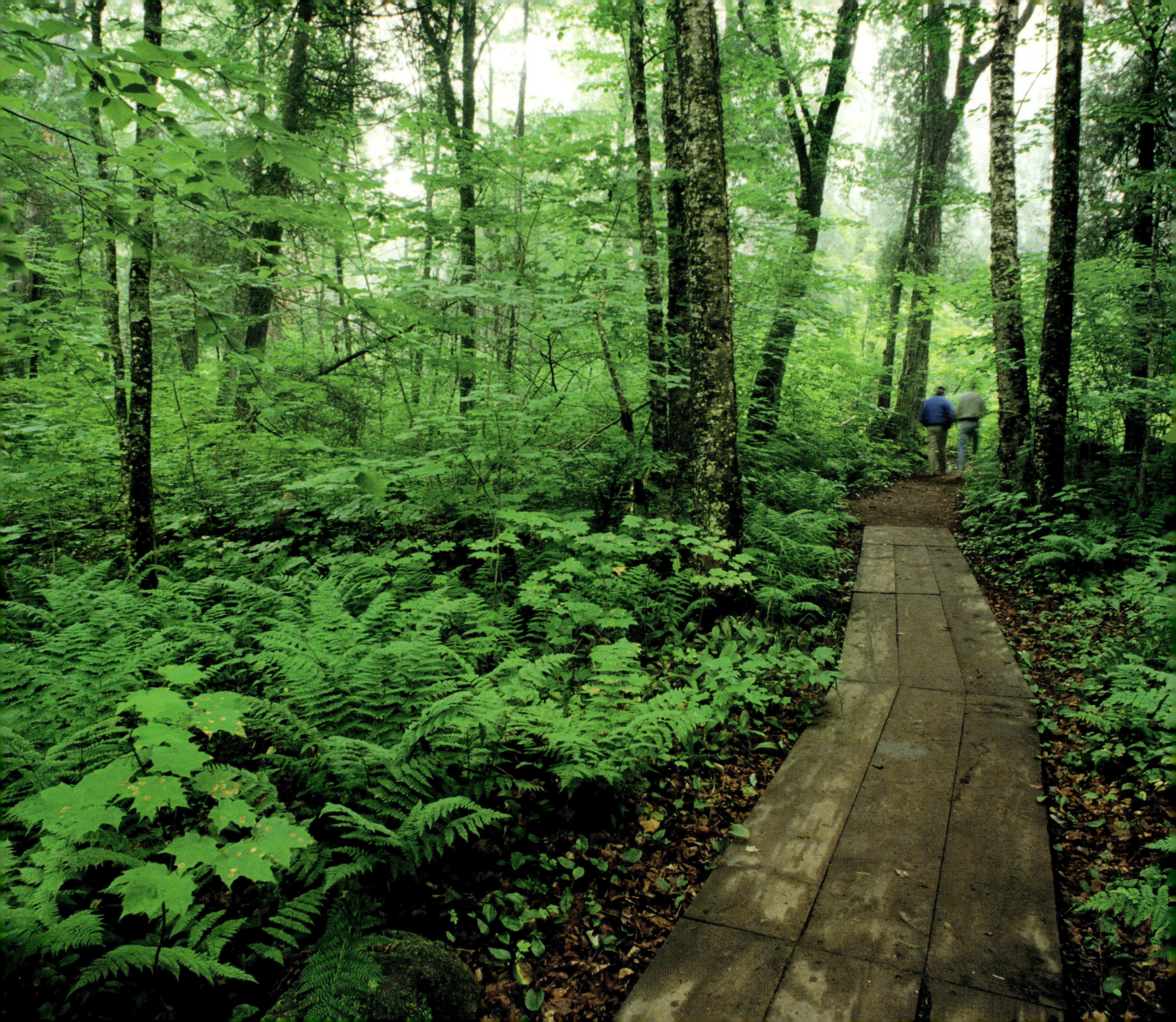

legacy of wanderers. From the bare rocks that peeked out from under the glaciers so long ago, life has swum, crawled, floated, flown, and drifted to these islands, weaving an intricate quilt of life. And the process is not over. Every wind, every wave can carry with it something new. Sometimes it is an exotic species such as the purple loosestrife that threatens Long Island or the gypsy moths that drifted to Basswood, Stockton, and other islands. Other times it is a species that, like an echo, was once here and now may be making a comeback.

On March 5, 2003 biologist Bill Route and others were traversing Sand Island as part of a deer survey, driving deer out of the brush to be counted by a researcher circling above in a plane. Working the southwestern part of the island on snowshoes, Route looked among the maze of deer tracks in the snow and saw something that had not been seen in the Apostles for more than 50 years: wolf tracks.

"The moment I saw them, there was no doubt in my mind what they were," says Route, who has worked with wolves in places like Voyageurs National Park and Alaska's Wrangell-St. Elias National Park. From the size and the directness of the gait, Route considered it a track from a single good-sized adult wolf. Wolves had been exterminated from Wisconsin in the late 1950s. The state's last wolf was bludgeoned to death with a tire iron just outside of Cornucopia in November of 1958. But they had since been working their way back into northern Wisconsin from Minnesota. As many as 350 wolves now live in the state, and several packs are known to range the Bayfield Peninsula. Just weeks before Bill Route's discovery on Sand Island there had been a confirmed wolf-killed deer on the park's mainland unit near the Mawikwe caves.

Coming across the track several times before it veered off his path, Bill Route followed the line of wolf prints with his eyes, witness to a sight that had not been seen among these islands for nearly a lifetime. The track line followed the deer trails, stopped to circle a log, crossed a beaver pond, then turned and vanished among the trees.

Above: The recovering forests of the islands hold rich rewards for the quiet and patient observer. The process of ecological renewal, or "re-wilding," provides visitors an opportunity to witness these changes first-hand.
Right: A boardwalk takes hikers over a boggy portion of the Tombolo Trail on Stockton Island.

Top, from left: Shelf fungus grows on rotting stumps and fallen timber. A tiny fly scours a hawkweed blossom looking for nectar. Water beetles check out an expired dragonfly on an island lagoon.
Right: Beads of dew on a spider's web contain tiny snapshots of their surroundings.
Below: Bog cranberries on Bear Island have recently dropped their blossoms.
Opposite: Ladyslippers on Stockton Island.

43

The Echoes of History

The *Mayfly* clatters through a tinsel-thin sheet of new ice as I shut off the engine, lift the prop, and drift into a small beach on the west side of Hermit Island. It is April, early to be on Lake Superior, but in a month there will be flocks of sailboats on the horizon, rainbows of kayaks pulled up on the beach. There will be footprints in the sand. Today there are no footprints, only the hieroglyphics of bird tracks. The island is deserted, just the way I want it. After all, I've come to search for a hermit.

Securing the boat on the beach, I bend back the branches and push my way into the woods. Hermit is not among the most-visited islands in the park. It has no maintained trails, no dock, no campground, and no interpretive signs to guide you. What it does have is a legend.

Remote, deserted islands have long sparked legends of hermits, dreams of solitude and self-reliance. From 1847 to 1861, a mysterious man lived that kind of life on this island, tending a small garden, making barrels to sell to fishermen, keeping mostly to himself. Like most good legends there are whispered claims of hidden treasure. Also like a good legend there are only scant clues—I have a 1954 newspaper article filled with secondhand accounts, and I've heard campfire stories. And then there is the name of this island found on old maps—Wilson's. But was that the man's first name or his last? How did he come to live here and why? What did he think about? What poetry or curse did he find in the silence of long winter nights?

I don't know if I'll find the answers but what would history be without a mystery? What would a collection of wild islands be without a hermit somewhere in its past and a story to ponder? It is that story, that mystery, and this old clipping, that draws me to again and again to Hermit Island searching for answers in the shadows.

Whatever answers there might be, the hermit was not the first to leave his footprints on the Apostles. Scattered on Manitou, Stockton, and other islands are at least 45 archaeological sites. Shards of bone and chips of pottery whisper of the Woodland Culture and other early nomadic people who hunted, fished, gathered, and traveled among the islands beginning with the melting of the glaciers. For most, the islands were just a stopover in a life of ceaseless movement. For the Ojibwe, who would come here sometime in the 1400s, the islands became a home.

"Centuries ago," says Damen Panek, an Ojibwe now working as a ranger with the National Park Service, "my people migrated here." They came, the oral tradition says, following a vision known as the "Seven Fires Prophecy." According to that prophecy, the Ojibwe would rise up from their lands in the East and follow the image of a sacred *Megis* (sea shell) that would lead them to a chosen spot, a land that would become, for them, the center of the universe. They would know the place by its shape—a turtle-shaped island—and by the gift of the food that grows on the water. After the prophesied seven stops their journey led them to *Moningwunakaunigh* (home of the yellow-breasted woodpecker), a place known today as Madeline Island.

"They knew they were coming to this place," Panek says. "This was no surprise. This was the place they were supposed to be going." What they found beneath the Megis was a difficult but fruitful place, with fish to net and white-tailed deer to hunt. There were birch trees for canoes and baskets. There were blueberries and nuts and mushrooms to gather. And there was wild rice, "the food that grows upon the water," its ripe grains whisked into the bottoms of canoes by the gentle drumbeat of gatherers passing through the marshes. Offerings of tobacco were given made from the bark of red willows, and the Ojibwe settled in to make a home.

The land and the lake fed the Ojibwe in body and spirit. The islands became woven into their lives and stories, sacred stories that were told of tricksters, of battles, and of how these islands were formed. Ojibwe Gerry DePerry tells it this way: "When the great spirit Winabojo was familiar with this part of the country, he noticed a huge beaver living in the bay. Wanting to capture that beaver, Winabojo took sticks and mud and built a large dam across the bay. But he didn't build it strong enough and the beaver escaped, making Winabojo so angry he took giant handfuls of the dam and threw them

Above: An old postcard was a tourist's memento of the island village of La Pointe.
Left: The Madeline Island Museum at La Pointe contains buildings and artifacts from the islands' diverse history.
Opposite: The quarry wall on Hermit Island is a permanent marker of human activity here.
Inset: Gifts lie before the gravestone of Ojibwe Chief Bezhiki on Madeline Island.

A postcard "souvenir" commemorated missionary and explorer Father Marquette's visit to La Pointe. The French missionaries played a major role in trade between native tribes and fur traders.

Below: Frederic Baraga, First Bishop of Marquette, was a French Jesuit missionary at La Pointe. He served among the natives and settlers until his death in 1868.

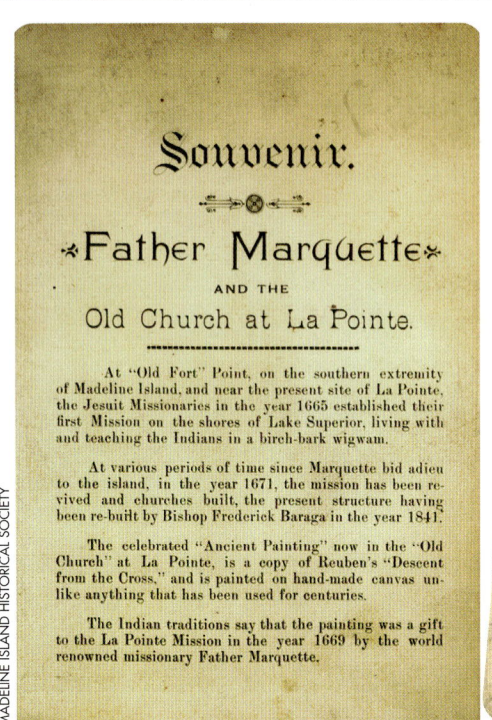

at the beaver as it swam away into the open lake. As far as he could see, Winabojo kept throwing handfuls of sand and rocks. Where each of those handfuls fell, there became an island." To this day, the Apostle Islands are just off shore of Chequamegon Bay, a rendition of the Ojibwe word "jagawaamikoong" or "soft beaver dam."

It was a difficult but good life on the bay for the Ojibwe for hundreds of years. But the influx of others beginning in the 1600s—Europeans following visions of their own, visions of timber and fur—would drastically alter that way of life. Treaties negotiated in 1854 split the Ojibwe, placing them on a pair of reservations on either side of the islands—Bad River to the south, and Red Cliff to the north. Still, while many other Native American people have been repeatedly uprooted and removed from their homelands, the Ojibwe have courageously clung to this place shown to them in their visions. From their chosen homeland along Chequamegon Bay, rangers like Damen Panek today help park visitors get a glimpse of the Ojibwe culture. Some, like Gerry DePerry tell the stories adding another link to the thread of words that reaches centuries back in time. And others, all through the region, work to honor and keep alive traditions of the people who came here following the Megis and discovered food, shelter, and a place they still call the center of their universe.

Beginning in the 1660s, these islands were at the center of another kind of universe: the burgeoning fur trade. Highly prized for fashioning the stylish top hats fancied by European gentlemen, beaver pelts were quickly becoming the "soft gold" that fueled a kind of rush into the nation's interior. Men and canoes poured down every river and creek. Two Frenchmen, Radisson and Groseillier, wintered over in 1658 on the shores of Chequamegon Bay near present-day Ashland. When they returned to Montreal in 1660 with a cargo of beaver pelts valued at $120,000, the fur trade had come to the islands.

The Apostles were perfectly situated to facilitate the "soft gold" rush. They held few beavers, but the true importance of the islands to the fur trade lay in their location. Like spokes on a wheel, trading routes radiated up and down nearly every navigable waterway leading into Lake Superior—Fish Creek, the Bad River, the Montreal, the St. Louis, and other tributaries became offshoots of the famous 4,000-mile "Voyageur Highway," the canoe and portage route that extended from Canada's interior, through the Great Lakes, to the mouth of the St. Lawrence River. Later, on the Brule River, a route would be discovered that linked Lake Superior with the Mississippi River drainage, opening up an immense web of trading routes to the West. In the middle of it all sat the Apostle Islands.

For nearly 200 years, the Apostles served as one of the major fur trade centers. As early as 1693, a fort and trading post was established at LaPointe on Madeline Island. Untold fortunes in fur moved through the region. Birchbark canoes up to 36 feet long manned by a dozen voyageurs with colorful toques flying, plied the big lake, filling morning mists with the strains of "En Boullant Rolle" and other French paddling songs. The air was abuzz with a mad mix of accents—French and British, Canadian, Native American and others—and filled with greed and hope, pipe smoke and dreams.

Of all the boom and bust cycles ridden out by

Upper left: The last building to house the Jesuit mission church on Madeline Island remembered on a postcard circa 1915.
Left: A typical scene at a trading post, depicted in this 19th century engraving. The North West Trading Company, owned by John Jacob Astor, operated a trading post on Madeline Island.

48

this region, the fur trade would boom the longest. Still, like pipe smoke in a stiff breeze, fur could not hold out forever. Changes in fashions and a shrinking beaver population led to a decline. As early as 1836, traders at LaPointe were eyeing other island resources in hopes of making up revenue shortfalls. But while voyageur canoes could haul mounds of fur, they were useless with fish, timber, and stone. Without reliable transportation to distant markets, the schemes would remain dead-end dreams. Then in 1855, the locks at Sault Saint Marie were opened, linking Superior to the ocean. The railroad whistled its way into Ashland in 1877, bringing with it access to the nation's interior. Once again, eyes turned to the resources awaiting on the islands.

For a time, those eyes focused on farming. "You can raise enough potatoes on two acres the first year to pay for 160 acres of land," the *Bayfield County Press* proclaimed of island farming. "An intelligent farmer can realize from ten acres of land more substantial benefit than he could from one hundred acres of Dakota land," the paper crowed, adding that even the "poorest land would produce 2½ tons of hay to the acre."

There were those who tried. As early as 1865, Richard McCloud filed a claim on a homestead farm on Basswood Island. By the late 1800s there were farms on Basswood, Sand, Hermit, Ironwood, and Oak, as well as a nursery of 20,000 fruit trees planted on Michigan Island by the light keeper. The *Bayfield County Press* bragged in 1877 of "a mammoth pumpkin, weighing 81 pounds, a snake cucumber, about four feet long." They were, the paper claimed the "products of Basswood Island, that wonderful place for farm products of mammoth proportion."

But all the local booster spirit in the world can't change thin soils or warm the cold winters. Weather took its toll. "A recent hail storm over on Bass Island," the paper dutifully reported, "utterly destroyed Joseph McCloud's fine garden. According to his own report, his cabbages were cut up fine as though they had been hashed through with a chopping knife." Difficult lake crossings took a toll as well. One island farmer turned his back on a flourishing crop after a particularly frightening crossing and said he would go back to farming on Michigan Island "as soon as nature builds him a bridge across there." No bridges were ever built. The winters stayed just as cold, and the dream of farming faded slowly away on the Apostle Islands.

While some were digging potatoes out of island soil, others were digging deeper, looking to harvest

Opposite: French voyageurs plied the shores of the upper Great Lakes, returning furs for trade in the East. Artist Howard Sivertson has researched and recreated numerous scenes, such as this one, of the voyageur expeditions.
Inset: Heavy loads of furs and supplies were carried across portage trails with the aid of a trumpline, or head strap, shown in a Remington drawing.

Above: Blocks of brownstone can still be seen at the quarry site on Hermit Island.
Opposite, top: The three-masted schooner was a typical "working ship" on Lake Superior in the late 1800s. Vessels like this hauled stone from Basswood, Hermit, and Stockton Islands. Lower: Apostle Islands National Lakeshore headquarters in Bayfield, originally the county courthouse, was built of island brownstone.

the very bones of the Apostle Islands. On my search for clues to the hermit, I step out of the trees and into an opening along the shore, a spot where the stones have a strange cut and cast. From the wave-rounded rocks on other parts of the island, I suddenly find myself among square-cut corners and sheer rock walls stripped with drill lines. Large rectangles of rock eight feet long and four feet deep sit stacked in silent heaps. Everything around me suggests the screech of hydraulics, the gunpowder smell of cracking rock. The air should vibrate with the shouts and grunts of sweat-soaked men, the twang of cables straining under immense weight. Yet the only sounds are a bird calling from the trees and the soft lap of the lake; the only movement, the slow dance of the grass. I have walked into the stone hallways of an old brownstone quarry.

From 1868 until the turn of the century, the Apostle Islands were the bedrock of the brownstone industry. Nine companies carved stone from at least four sites on three of the islands, sending the brownstone bones of the Apostles to distant cities where they would be used to build banks, schools, libraries, and railway stations. As with every resource-based industry to touch the Apostles, the brownstone boom was fueled by the whims and fashions of far-away cities. And in this case the fabled kicking hooves of Mrs. O'Leary's cow.

In the wake of the 1871 Chicago fire, reportedly touched off by a lantern knocked over in a milk barn, architects sought a building material to symbolize the country's strength, resolve, and unbreakable will, as well as one less flammable than the wooden slats of frontier towns. They found it in the brown-swirled bedrock of the Apostle Islands.

First on Basswood and later on both Stockton and Hermit, armies of workers cleared brush, felled trees, and peeled back the soil to reveal the stone bones of the islands. Originally by blasting and later with steam-powered drills—but mostly with sweat, strain, and muscle—mountains of rock were quarried from the islands. Exact figures may lay in long-lost ledgers, but yearly shipments from the Stockton

Island quarry—the largest operation among the Apostles—have been estimated as high as 285,000 cubic feet.

Prized for its coloring and its strength, Apostle Island brownstone left the quarries on the strong backs of tugs like the *Favorite*, the *Starlight*, and the *Minnie V*, only to reappear in the rising walls of the Milwaukee Courthouse, the Chicago Tribune building, the First Methodist Episcopal Church of Duluth, Ashland's Vaughn Library, and the Bayfield County Courthouse—the same building that today houses the headquarters of the Apostle Islands National Lakeshore.

A hundred men worked the rock at Basswood earning a dollar a day and often spending it just as quickly. The *Bayfield Press* reports several instances of the "Basswood Island boys" working off a case of restlessness in the local taverns with "numerous exclamations of "yaverly, labona, Stockholm and King Georgia" fueled by weeks of hard work, island isolation, and the "salubrious effect of John Barleycorn."

There was, however, a softer side to quarry life. Families sometimes joined the workers at the hastily cobbled shacks rising around the rock pits, their presence blunting the hard edge of island existence. A baby boy was born to a quarry worker and his wife on Basswood Island in 1871. But a birth and a few lace curtains could not compensate for the often brutally harsh conditions. On Christmas Eve of 1893, one Mrs. McCrea from the camp on Basswood set out with two companions for some last-minute holiday shopping at Bayfield, three miles across the ice. Caught in a blizzard on their return trip, the party was swirled in an impenetrable shroud of wind and snow. They struggled through the deepening snow, stumbling with their arms full of packages, ribbons, and bows. With the island cloaked by the storm and the trail obliterated by the wind, they soon lost their way. Finally, cold, lost, and exhausted, Mrs. McCrea sat down to rest. That's where her husband would find her hours later, clinging to life, unable to talk. It was a solemn Christmas on the island, as Mrs. McCrea died in her husband's arms less than a mile from her island home.

A place that swallowed people in storms or

Inset: The Cedar Bark Lodge, built on Hermit Island by quarry owner Frederick Prentice in the 1890s, long since disintegrated.

Below: The Schroeder Lumber Co. built a railway the length of Outer Island to haul logs off the island to the lake where they were corralled into immense rafts and towed to the mainland.

swept them away in boats must have seemed the very edge of the world to the young bride of Frederick Prentice, the 70-year-old rock baron of the Excelsior Brownstone Quarry on Hermit Island. In the 1890s, near the end of the brownstone boom, Prentice had a fine Victorian-style home built on a ledge overlooking the quarry, sparing no expense on its finery. Despite his efforts, legend says his bride, straight from the bright lights of the big city, took one look at the Cedar Bark Lodge and its isolated setting and left forever. The structure sat mostly empty over the years, until it finally moldered into the ground with the dreams of Frederick Prentice.

The advent of steel building materials and a change in architectural tastes soon spelled the end of the brownstone heyday in the Apostles. The quarries all went silent.

But other sounds were already ringing out across the islands—the rasp of saws and cries of "timber!" An 1857 survey showed the islands as a nearly unbroken virgin forest of hemlock and pine, oak, birch, and maple. That would soon change.

Commercial logging began in the 1880s. Proximity to the water made for cheap transportation. Hills and gullies easily funneled cut logs toward the lake. And the island forests fell quickly. By 1850 Oak Island was the site of a cordwood operation supplying wood for the steamboats. Stockton had five camps including Trout Point, which housed 100 lumberjacks. A Basswood Island camp held a dozen horses and 50 men cutting wood used for everything from heating the Bayfield high school to constructing piers in England.

First it was the pine, used in construction and for railroad cross-ties. Next the hemlock fell, its bark valued in the tanning of leather. Last to go were the hardwoods, oak and maple. Some islands

Left: The Island View Hotel in Bayfield in about 1900.
Below: Weary faces line the walls of a crudely built lumber camp mess hall.

were shaved repeatedly—Otter Island in 1903 and again in 1957; Sand Island in 1898, 1906, again in the 1940s and once more in the 1970s.

The cut was staggering. In 1897, 350,000 board feet of pine were taken off Rocky Island. In the 1890s, two million board feet were removed from Basswood. Reports in the *Bayfield Press* claim that in July of 1920, 15 million board feet from the previous winter's cut on Oak were towed to Ashland. Chequamegon Bay became a mill pond. Immense rafts of logs, some more than a mile across, were pulled toward Ashland, Washburn, and Bayfield by tugs like the *Butterfield*.

Fortunes grew faster than heaps of sawdust, empires built of wood for men like local lumber baron R.D. Pike. But those empires were hoisted

Right and below: On Mawikwe Bay, a steam-powered hauler with tracks and sled runners towed logs across the frozen lake.

on the backs of men doing difficult and dangerous work, a danger magnified by the islands themselves. In 1913, a crew at the Schroeder Lumber Camp on Stockton staged a strike, stopping their saws until a resident doctor was brought to the island. There was no such medical care on Oak Island. In January 1929, the *Bayfield Press* reported that "Ed Mkei (sic), lumberjack at Smith's lumber camp #6 . . . was driving down a steep hill with a big load of logs on a sleigh; the sleigh jumped out of the rut and smashed into a stump, throwing him off the load and under the falling logs. His left leg was broken below the knee." With the ice too thick to boat him off the island and too thin for horse-drawn sleigh, the lumberjacks improvised. "A rope of some 200 feet in length was tied about the body of one of the men who went ahead of the party . . . to test the ice. If he went through, his companions would endeavor to pull him back to safety and then seek a safer route. By dint of much careful testing . . . the party finally brought the injured man to this city where he was taken by train to an Ashland hospital."

Some thought the timber would last forever. The *Bayfield Press* claimed in 1877 that "cord wood, pine logs, oak timber, steamboat wood . . . are (our) staple products, and the supply is unlimited." But it was not unlimited. The pine was mostly gone by 1908. The hardwood heyday began to dim by the 1930s, though some cutting would continue even into the 1970s.

The toll was immense. The fur trade had lasted longer. The brownstone carvers had dug deeper. But no other resource boom has left as deep and lasting a footprint on the Apostle Islands as logging. It changed the islands' ecology, both from the cutting and the fires that inevitably followed – a single 1934 fire charred more than 4,000 acres of Oak Island. Fires also blazed on Outer, Stockton and other islands. By the early 1900s, so many island fires raged that lighthouse logs often record "sounding for the smoke." It may have changed their political fortunes—a National Park Service representative visited the islands in 1931 and found only stumps and slash heaps, delaying for decades its national lakeshore status. It even changed the name of one island: Cat Island was known as "Hemlock" until the loggers stripped it of that species.

Forests still fringe the Apostles—deep, green, leafy forests of oak and birch and pine. Deep in such forest, it can still feel wild, and it is, but the islands are ecologically different from the pre-logging days. Today we can get a look back in time to the logging history of the islands with visits to old logging camps, and by finding old saws and stumps in the grass. But glimpses of the old forests are harder to come by. Only Devils Island and Raspberry Island, designated as lighthouse reserves, escaped the saw. Small areas around the other lighthouses were also spared. Hike today on the north end of Outer, among scattered pines so big three people can barely ring them with their

Above: Logging operations at Lullabye Lumber Company saw the advent of increased mechanization.
Left: The contractor's truck remains, a rusting witness to regeneration of the forest around it.

Above and right: A few optimistic souls attempted farming on the islands. The thin layer of soil yielded only a few bumper crops before the enterprise had to be given up.

Lower right: Island dwellers skiing to school in the 1920s with pillowcases serving as backpacks.

arms, or walk quietly through the fern-speckled shadows of the trees near the Sand Island Light, and you may glimpse the forest that once stood on these islands. But even then, it is only a glimpse.

The spring sun is already skimming the horizon by the time I work my way back to my boat on the shore. I've hiked the whole island and found not even the smallest glimpse of the hermit's history. The old newspaper article, nearly in tatters now from so many trips, chatters about an all-day fist fight with "King" Bell of Madeline Island, the loser to be banished to another island. It speaks of Wilson's days with the fur trade and drops hints of romance and adventure. Yet the article was written more than 90 years after the hermit's death, and with only the wispiest ties to verifiable fact.

In truth, no one knows for sure where his cabin was, what trails he walked, or how he lived or died. And a part of me likes it that way. The lack of solid leads lets me walk the island over and over, wondering, "Is this the clearing? Is this where his garden was?" I sit on stumps and try to paint the picture in my mind—his one-room cabin with its crude furniture, a burlap sack stuffed with feathers for a pillow, a single book, perhaps *The Whole Duty of Man*, the book mentioned in the old newspaper story. I watch a fishing boat far off, trailing a puff of gulls like white smoke, and wonder what voices Wilson must have imagined in the galleys of passing ships when the ice finally broke after a long winter. I wonder other things, too. Did he sing while he gardened? Did he get lonely?

Who among us has not daydreamed about a solitary life on a wild island? There is, I think, a little bit of the hermit in all of us. Sitting along the shore I wonder, what in my own life could I leave behind to live alone on this tiny, 774-acre island? What would I miss—my family, ice cream, the scratchy sound of baseball games on the radio at night?

I may never know, but then, there is much more to an island's history than what you find in books and archives. Mystery has its place among these islands, too. A strong breeze comes up off the lake bending the birch trees like question marks, but as I sit watching the last light fade into the lake, no answers are whispered to me on the wind.

Above: A pioneer cabin succumbs gradually to nature, one of many such dwellings once inhabited throughout the islands.
Left: The excursion boat *Chippewa*, advertised in this 1960s postcard, carried both tourists and residents between Bayfield and the islands.

Sand Island Voices

There was Francis Shaw, the "Emperor of Sand Island," who raised potatoes and goats on "a good snug farm" and once lifted 3,200 pounds of lake trout in a single haul. There was light keeper Emmanuel Luick, who watched in horror as the 373-foot steamer *Sevona* broke up on a shoal, taking seven men to their graves. There was Burt Hill, who for decades with his wife Anna Mae, was the heart and soul of the island—postmaster, store clerk, farmer, fisherman, telephone operator, rum runner, and handy man.

There are voices on Sand Island. Nowhere on these islands do the echoes of history ring more clearly. Two settlements once stood here. There was a post office, a county road, a cooperative store, even telephone service until a boat severed the line to the mainland. People lived here, mostly Scandinavian immigrants who came to fish and farm. They worked clearing fields, planting crops and pulling nets. They battled storms. They laughed and danced at picnics on the school grounds. They lived, in short, an island life—rich, difficult, and seemingly timeless. Once, the lighthouse keeper from the north end of the island visited the settlement at East Bay to find "the people over there had lost track of time and did not know either the day or date."

There is still that sense of timelessness on Sand Island. Step off the Park Service dock at East Bay and you hike past the rusted shell of a 1932 Model A once owned by Gertrude Wellish. She called her cabin "Plenty Charm," and it still graces the shoreline. The rubble of the "Herring King Cabin" lies somewhere in the brush, its roof made from the upturned hull of a fishing boat that burned on a calm day in 1917. A faint trail to the

Above: Burt Hill at the offices of the *Bayfield County Press*.
Center: Fred Hansen's family members pose for a photo on the Sand Island dock; one seated in Fred's boat, *Lady Grace*.
Lower left: Sand Island families worked hard and had few comforts, but they had much to enjoy in island life on Lake Superior.

north leads into the open fields of the old Noring farm, where a rusty hayrick, a well, and a tumbled brick chimney speak of the "huge strawberries," vegetable gardens, hay fields, livestock, and orchard that once stood here. Peer through the brush and listen for the peal of the old school bell, calling to class the 13 students of teacher Evelyn Cowie. The one-room "northernmost of Wisconsin's schools" operated from 1910 until 1928, and its foundation is still visible in the grass.

Sand Island has the longest continuous history of human habitation of all the islands included in the Apostle Islands National Lakeshore. The population of Sand Island peaked at about a hundred residents between 1911 and 1918. Soon afterward, difficult economic times, the distance to markets, medical care, and jobs, and a changing world, led family after family to leave the island. By October of 1944, the *Ashland Daily Press* proclaimed "Sand Island Deserted First Time In Half a Century."

The people are gone, but their stories live on—well-documented in the writings of Sam Fifield. The former Wisconsin lieutenant governor built Camp Stella, a resort for hay fever sufferers, on the west side of the island, and often wrote of island life. And stories are told in the diaries of Fred Hansen, who came to the island with his family in 1893. For 25 years he wrote daily notes of dances and drownings, cutting wood, and lifting nets. There are hundreds of old black and white photographs in the National Park Service —Axel Anderson with his huge draft horses, Burt Hill lifting nets or lounging beneath a shade tree, the huge hay stacks at the Moe farm.

Still, the best way to get a glimpse of what life was like on Sand Island is to make the crossing in a small boat, hike the trails, stand in the clearings, search for the old cabins, climb the lighthouse tower, and listen. There are voices on Sand Island.

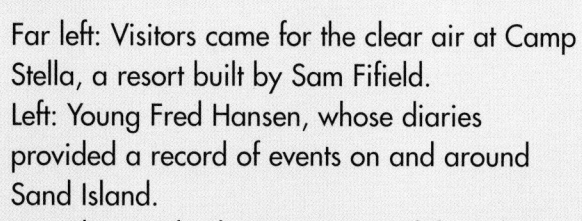

Far left: Visitors came for the clear air at Camp Stella, a resort built by Sam Fifield.
Left: Young Fred Hansen, whose diaries provided a record of events on and around Sand Island.
Top: Three girls play jump-rope while a dozen other students pose on the steps at the Sand Island School.

A Keeper's Tale

KEEPER'S LOG, May 28: Skies: Clear. Winds: 15 to 20 knots from the NE. Waves: 3 to 4 feet shimmering like shattered rainbows where they smash against the shore. Vessel Traffic: a single fishing boat bobbing in the waves. Temperature: 55 degrees. A lone gull rides the wind, tips its wings, and then vanishes around the point.

It is just an entry in my old spiral notebook. Nothing like an official keeper's log has been required at the Raspberry Island Light for over 50 years. Still, a person can dream, and where better to dream than in a lighthouse standing alone on an island?

The Raspberry Island Light stands 80 feet above the lake at the southern tip of the island. Seventy-six steps lead up from dock to the grounds and the keeper's quarters, an elegant, stately structure that, at first glance, resembles a plantation home more than a light keeping station. There are flower boxes that in high summer will be nodding with orange day lilies and purple pansies, and garden walks upon which visitors—as many as 8,000 per year—will file past rows of carrots, onions, and squash. There are grape arbors and berry bushes, and, once I set it up, even a croquet course on the neatly trimmed grounds. All of that and a view—not of wild, white-capped horizons but of blue-black islands and mainland hills—only add to the country club feeling. But for more than 80 years this was a working lighthouse, its heart the 40-foot square-boxed tower rising from its center and capped with its glass-eyed turret.

First lit on July 20, 1863, the Raspberry Island Light saw a string of keepers in its day, men like Francis Jacker, Lee Benton, Seth Snow, and others—16 keepers in its 84 years of manned history. Now, for a night or two, it is my turn. For a few days before the arrival of the seasonal ranger, who'll spend the summer on the island, the National Park Service has dubbed me the "unofficial volunteer keeper" of the Raspberry Island Light. The job comes with slim duties. Frankly, there isn't much for a keeper, official or otherwise, to do here anymore. The light, once a Fifth Order Fresnel lens hand-crafted in France and lit every night by a keeper trudging up the tower, is now a plastic beacon triggered by an automatic solar-powered timing system. Without so much as the touch of a human hand, the light blinks on at dusk and snaps off at the appointed hour after sunrise. The best thing I can do is to keep watch over it all.

There is no coal to haul for the steam boilers that once gave breath to the 10-inch steam whistle which bellowed from the red brick fog signal building next to the quarters. There are no wicks to trim, no brass fittings to polish. I am simply here as the self-appointed inspector of sunsets and to greet any early Memorial Day visitors. But more than that, I am here to dream of the time when these lights were still tended by human hands. I am here to remember the keepers.

The Apostles have long been both a blessing and a curse for lake sailors. The deep natural harbors were attractive ports. In storms, even open lake boats still run for a lee among the islands, glad to wait things out in the protection they offer. Yet the lure of leeward bays and a safe haven does not come without the risks of hidden shoals and uncharted rocky shorelines. The bones of more than twenty known wrecks wreathe the islands, among them the fire-charred hull of the *Noque Bay* in Julian Bay sands off Stockton Island; the *Lucerne*, which came to an icy end off Long Island with three crew members frozen to death in its masts; and the ongoing mystery of the vanished *Manistee*.

As a hedge against those risks, a trail of lights was built early among the islands. The earliest—Michigan Island Light (1857), LaPointe Light on Long Island (1858), and Raspberry Island Light (1863)—were built to guide ships into and among the Apostles. Vessels came loaded with dreams and high hopes, following the lights to ports on Madeline Island and at Bayfield. Later, as the main shipping routes began to bypass those ports, other lights were added—Outer Island (1874), Sand Island (1881), and Devils Island (1891)—to warn vessels away from the islands as new shipping routes crisscrossed the lake to and from busier ports in Duluth, Superior, and Thunder Bay.

Whether to guide ships in among the islands or safely lead them away, the lighthouses of the Apostles were in essence the first marked trail across this part of Lake Superior, a trail of lights. Each beam was a unique blaze in the dark—the steady red-eyed stare of Devils Light visible 21 miles out; the clear white, every-90-second flash of Raspberry Island Light; the green flicker of the Chequamegon Point

Above: The stately residence at Raspberry Island was built to accommodate two keepers and their families.
Opposite: A seasonal ranger gives visitors a tour of the Raspberry Island Lighthouse and grounds. Raspberry is the most popular of the Apostle Islands lights.
Insets: The National Park Service is collecting furnishings and artifacts to install in the light station to give tourists a feeling for the life of the keepers and their families.

🜋 61

The Fresnel (FRAYnel) lens on Devils Island was restored and returned to the tower after having been removed by the Coast Guard in 1989. The light station, now maintained by the National Park Service, is listed in the National Register of Historic Places. Opposite: Devils Lighthouse.

Light, the second of two lights on Long Island. Behind each beam there stood a keeper.

The key rattles in the lock, and the heavy wooden door to the keeper's quarters swings open with a tired creak. My footsteps echo heavily in the nearly empty quarters and then stop as I stand quietly, letting my eyes adjust to the dimness.

Just a few decades ago this would have been a very different scene. There would have been sunlight streaming in through the spotless windows, and wildflowers in a vase on the sill. The aroma of baking bread or freshly ground coffee might have wafted through the sunlit air. At this time of morning, keeper Benton might have just finished breakfast after extinguishing the light for the day, sitting bleary-eyed at the table in his suspenders while his new wife Bess clattered dishes in the sink and kept an eye on Benton's son Harold as he played with a handful of colorful beach pebbles strewn across the floor.

Life at a lighthouse was a combination of dedication and repetition, its cadence set by the weather and the needs of the light. The keeper (sometimes with his family, sometimes alone) came on duty in April, or as soon as the ice went out, carried across the water to the station by tenders like the *Marigold* or *Ameranth*. They would stay until just before freeze-up in December. In between, there were grounds to

⚓ 63

Inset: Robert Carlson was the Michigan Island Lightkeeper from 1893 to 1898.
Below: Late afternoon light bathes the buildings, light towers and rock cliffs on Devils Island.

tend, buildings to maintain, and wood to chop. Quarters had to be kept up and ready for inspection at a moment's notice. Keepers often fished to supplement the average annual wage of $600. They chopped wood and hunted. But the main duty—the most important element of life at the lighthouse—was to keep the light shining.

All of the Apostle Island lights were eventually outfitted with Fresnel lenses, ornate, almost chandelier-like creations that used a series of bull's-eye prisms to focus the beam of light and throw it out over the lake. The lenses are beautiful.

They were powerful, capable of tossing light many times farther than simple reflection lamps. They were also finicky, and needed almost constant maintenance. Lit from within by a lamp with up to four wicks, the light was fueled by kerosene that had to be hauled each day up the tower. The keepers meticulously trimmed each wick to provide a clear, smokeless flame, a process which earned them the nickname "Wickies." Kerosene smoke could soot the lens and the windows, dimming the light, so every pane of glass and every prism had to be polished regularly. "We cleaned the lens quite a bit," Vern Barningham, the keeper at several Apostle lights wrote. "Twice a week at least. Polished the lens. Cleaned the prism, kept it going."

Some of the lights were "fixed," sending out a steady, unblinking beam. Others were outfitted with massive spinning mechanisms that would turn the lens, causing it to "flash" a unique pattern of light to the sailors on the lake. Keepers of flashing lights also had to tend to and clean the spinning mechanisms with their chains of weights often weighing upwards of 100 pounds, winding them like giant old-fashioned clocks every three hours. Then there were sweeping and dusting, touching up the paint, and other minor repairs. By regulation all had to be in order by 10 a.m. each day, tested and ready for the keeper to ascend the tower once again a half an hour before sunset to light the light. In shifts with an assistant keeper, or all by himself if necessary, the keeper would then work through the night, ensuring a strong and steady beam until half an hour after sunrise each morning when the light would be extinguished, cleaned, and prepared for the next night.

It could be a monotonous schedule. The drumbeat-like repetition in the 1897 Raspberry Island logbook reflects that monotony:

07/11/97 Thermometer at noon: 65 degrees. Done all that was necessary: Sunday.

07/12/97 Thermometer at noon: 78 degrees. Cleaning lens and clock and painting inside the tower.

07/13/97 Temperature at noon: 82 degrees. Cleaning windows and washing floor.

Because it was nearer the mainland than others, Raspberry Island Light seemed less remote, but even here a keeper could go most of the summer with little company. "Tug *Daisy* brought an excursion party," Jacker wrote in his logbook for August 11, 1887. "They were the first visitors of the season."

Such remoteness could rub some people the wrong way. On Outer Island, the most distant Apostle Island station, things nearly came to blows between keepers in 1874. "I have lived in a perfect hell . . ." Keeper O.K. Hall wrote, complaining of life with his assistant John Drouillard. "He abuses me with the most profane language a man can utter, from no cause or provocation, and threatened to give me a thrashing. I caught him asleep on his watch and since then, he has lived in one part of the house and I in the other."

Above: Sand Island is relatively easy to reach by kayak, since it is on one of the nearest islands to the mainland.
Left: The Sand Island Lighthouse, built of native sandstone, is the most picturesque of the Apostle Islands lights.

65

Above: A second, taller light tower was added at Michigan Island light station after it was determined that the original lighthouse wasn't tall enough.

But solitude could be more than just irritating; it could be downright dangerous, as Jacker himself found out. For years he had been requesting an assistant. "In case of an emergency, no assistance is available . . ." he would write in pleas to superiors—pleas that were repeatedly turned down. Then, a September 1887 storm caught him out in his disabled sailboat, leaving him stranded on Oak Island, cold, hungry and "but scantily dressed" for three days. For three days, the Raspberry Light went untended. He was finally rescued by a passing boater. An assistant, Jacker's brother Edward, was assigned to the station the very next year.

"Live long enough around these isolated light stations," one Lake Superior keeper wrote, "and you'll be seeing mermaids . . . on the rocks and hear them singing." Keepers and their families did whatever they could to ward off visions of mermaids and other hallucinations of isolation. At Raspberry Island they tended lush flower gardens that scented the summer breeze, their work punctuated with the clack of croquet balls as the children or visitors played on the side lawn. The keeper's logs mention "a sewing circle" and "nice little parties." There were baseball games, music including an organ and dances at Sand Island, and guitars at the Michigan Island Light. In 1876 the U.S. Lighthouse Service began a program of portable libraries that circulated among the more remote light stations. These contained books like *Newcomb's Astronomy*, and an eight-volume set of *The Library of Choice Literature*.

To some, the simple pleasures of island living were enough, like a Fourth of July bonfire. "We'd gather logs . . . and build a fort. Build it as high as we could and filled it with driftwood," remembers Edna Lane Sauer, daughter of a Michigan Island light keeper. "In the evening, when it was getting dark, we'd go down. Dad would light it . . . they must have seen it all over the Apostle Islands because we'd make it a big one. We never lacked for something to do. We were always happy and busy."

For all the concerns about loneliness and drudgery, there was one thing that keepers feared more on their remote outpost islands—a Lake Superior storm.

One o'clock.
Two o'clock.

As much as I'd like to, I have decided not to go up into the tower until just before sunset, the time the keeper would kindle the light for the evening. For whatever frayed thread of logic there might be to holding to the old schedule, I will try to keep to the appointed rounds. With the quarters opened up and cleaned, the croquet wickets in place on the grounds and tested, I watch a ray of sunlight work its way across the floorboards. Then I sit in the sun to read an account of one legendary Lake Superior gale: the storm of September 2, 1905.

"Cleaning, trimming lamps and lens. Tending signal," begins the log entry that day, written in the hand of Outer Island keeper John Irvine. "A terrible gale blowing from the NE."

Set 25 miles out from the mainland, Outer Island is like a clenched fist directly in the path of Superior's worst fury. Storms often rock the island. In 1874, the first season of its operation, a big storm had swept away the dock. In a 1916 gale, the keeper recorded, "Tower is shaking very bad." On September 2, 1905, things were stacking up for another big blow. "The biggest sea I have seen since I have been at the station which is eight years," Irvine wrote, and then braced for the worst.

It came soon enough. "About 2:30 pm sighted a schooner about 2 miles NE of station." It was the *Pretoria*. The 338-foot wooden schooner loaded with iron ore had been in tow behind the steamer *Venezuela* some 30 miles northeast of Outer Island when the violent waves tore the cable, leaving the *Pretoria* and her crew of 10 completely at the mercy of the wind. Captain Charles Smart had tried everything—raising the sails, dragging the

Above: The Outer Island Lighthouse is the most remote of the Apostle Islands Lights. Built in 1874, this light was constructed to guide ships past the islands.

67

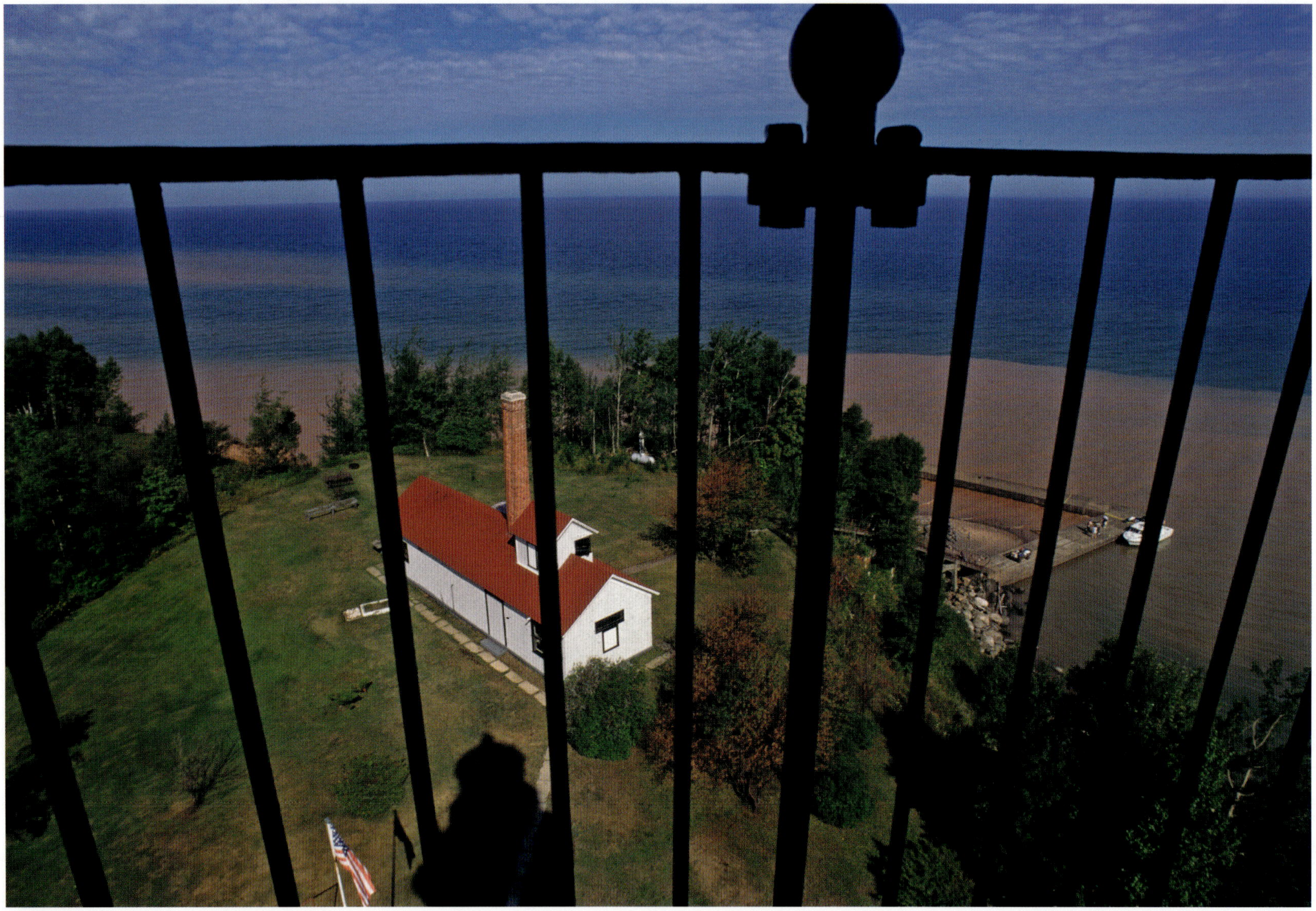

anchor—but against the fury of the storm nothing seemed to make a difference. Without power, the *Pretoria* was being pushed slowly but inexorably toward disaster on the jagged rocks of Outer Island. At just after 4 p.m., within full view of Keeper Irvine watching from the tower, the ship began breaking up. Just off Outer Island, the crew threw themselves into the single tiny life raft and made a desperate lunge for shore.

"I the keeper," Irvine would write, "hurried down with a white flag in my hand and a piece of rope to render what assistance I could." The "assistance" that John Irvine would render would later be called "almost superhuman" by one newspaper account. With no regard for his own safety, the 60-year-old keeper plunged again and again into the maelstrom, braving the mountainous crash of frigid waves to pull frantic men, one by one from the freezing water. It was too much to save them all, but he did what he could. Five men were drowned, bashed mercilessly against the rocks. Five others, including Captain Smart, were pulled from the storm by what must have seemed a vision, the keeper of the Outer Island Light.

Nearly a hundred years later, at exactly one half hour before sunset, I climb the winding staircase to the top of tower at the Raspberry Island Light. As I step through the small trap door, the horizons open suddenly like the wings of some blue-tinged bird.

There is no storm on this day. The lake is soft blue and endless. For all the luxuries of the grounds and the flower beds, this is the spot from which it is easiest to put yourself into the brass-buttoned uniform of a keeper, to see through his eyes. On how many days like this one did Francis Jacker or Lee Benton peer out at the same view? How often on days like this did the feeling of fortune at being up here, alone with the lake and the breeze, well up in their chests? How often were all the rigors and solitude of lighthouse keeping, and

Above: Emmanuel Luick with his sister-in-law, left, his son and his wife Oramill (right) at Devils Island Light. Luick was the keeper at Sand Island Light for 29 years.
Inset: LaPointe Light on Long Island was erected to guide ships into Chequamegon Bay.
Opposite: The view from the Outer Island Lighthouse, after a storm had stirred up sediment offshore.

⚓ 69

Right: There were three houses for the keepers and assistant keeper at Devils Island Light Station. Below: Chequamegon Point Light on Long Island.

the storms —for a time, at least—forgotten?

Raspberry Island Light was last lit by human hands in 1947. Some island lights had already been automated—Sand Island in 1921, Michigan Island Light in 1943. Others—Outer Island in 1961, Long Island's LaPointe Light in 1964—would soon follow. The last to be automated in the Apostles was the Devils Island Light. When its beam flashed on for the first time without the touch of human hands in 1978, it signaled the end of over a century of lighthouse keepers in these islands. Automated lights were cheaper and easier to maintain. Advances in ship navigation devices were quickly making blinking lighthouses obsolete.

Yet something was lost as well: a history, a way of life, the pride of the keepers and their families that stood behind the beam. Today the lighthouses of the Apostles are maintained by the National Park Service, forming the greatest collection of lighthouses in any national park unit. Work will soon begin to restore the Raspberry keeper's quarters to its 1924 condition. The Raspberry Island Light is the most visited light station in the Apostles, and the restored station will be a showcase for the park. A major stabilization project was recently completed to safeguard the buildings from the crumbling banks.

On a remote island, such work is difficult and expensive, yet vital. There will always be dusty old black-and-white photographs of keepers and their families. There will always be stories told in books or around campfires. But the best way to get a hint of what it meant to be a keeper at an Apostle Island light is to walk in the same footsteps; to climb the steps to the tower and gaze out across the lake—something that can only be done if the National Park Service can keep these light stations standing.

From the top of the Raspberry Island Light, I lean on the rail and scan the lake with my binoculars. Once these were busy waters. In 1903, the Devils Island keeper counted 120 ships in sight in a single glance. Today there is just one small excursion boat making its way along the far shore. I follow its progress until just before dark, then make a final entry in my own keeper's log:

May 28th, sunset. Sky: cloudless. Wind NE at 5 knots. Just a single ship in sight, its lights flickering on like colored stars low along the horizon. Temperature: 51 degrees. Waves: 1 to 2 feet. Mermaids: None yet, but I'll keep my eyes peeled.

Left: Inside the Outer Island Lighthouse, visitors can climb the ornate spiral staircase to the light.

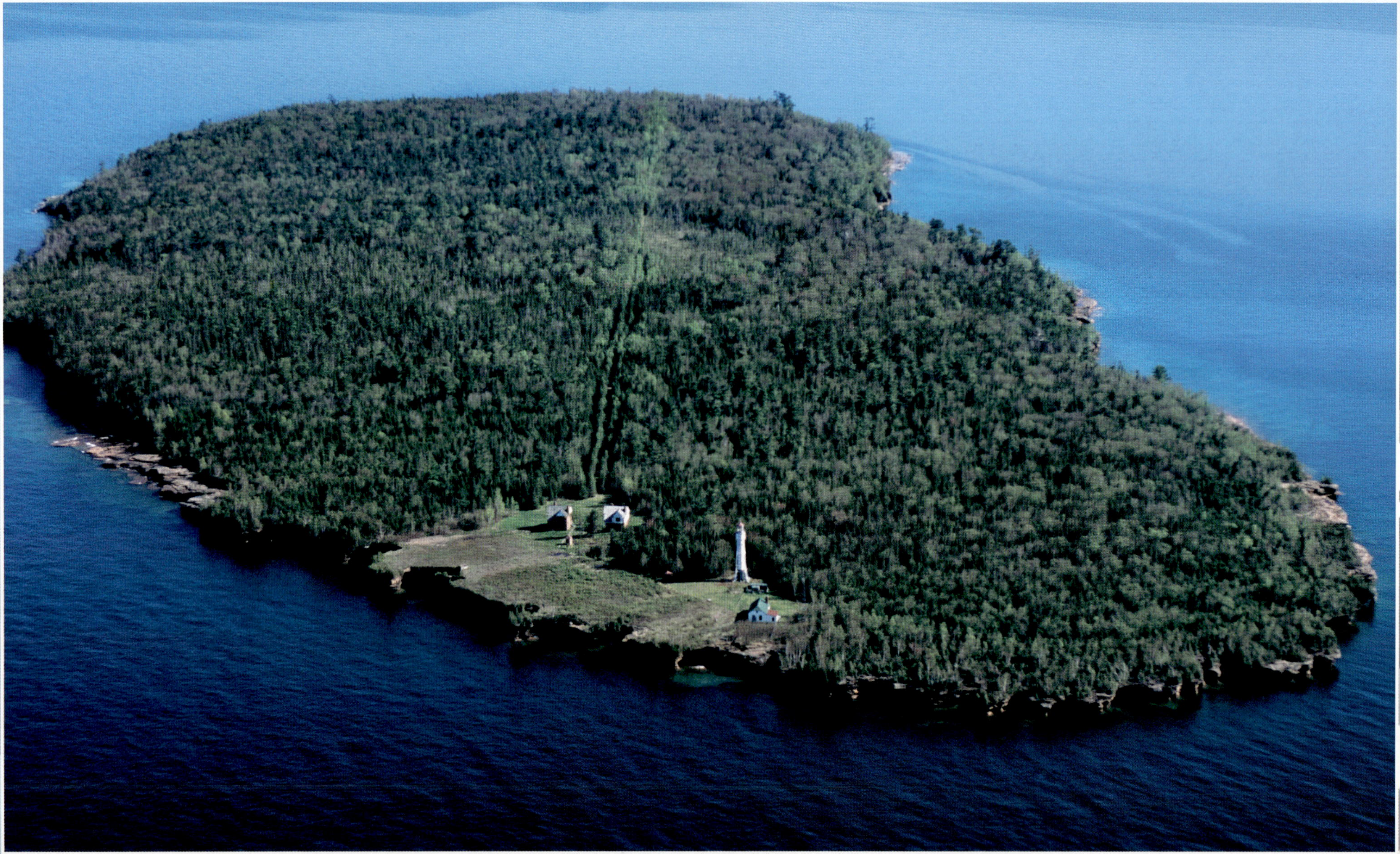

A shelf of Devils Island sandstone extends the view on the northeastern edge of the island.

Lifting Nets

Four-thirty. The day's first light is not yet a hint on the horizon when Marty Erickson frees the lines and steps lightly onto the deck of the *Donna Belle* as she clears the dock of the Bodin Fishery at Bayfield. The smells of diesel fumes, fish guts, and coffee swirl with the lake breeze as I scramble for a place to stand among the tangle of ropes and tools and fish boxes. "Settle in," Marty shouts over the thrum of the engines. "It's a two-hour run to the first set." I grab a spot on an upturned bucket, sip my coffee, and hunker down to ward off the chill. We are off to do something that fishermen have done for centuries among these islands—we are going to lift the nets.

Fishing has been a part of the Apostles for as long as humans have walked the shores and paddled the waters. Archaeologists have unearthed thousands of fish bones in prehistoric sites on Manitou Island. The Ojibwe worked the shallows with nets spun of willow bark and nettle fibers. Fish stretched the bellies of the French voyageurs during the fur trade, and when the beaver population began to decline, dealers at the LaPointe trading post first turned to fish in hopes of bolstering sagging profits. As early as 1836, they experimented with shipping 200 barrels of fish. Two thousand barrels were shipped the next year, and five thousand by 1839.

Up against fluctuating markets, transportation problems, and the vagaries of Lake Superior weather, the transition from fur to fish was far from smooth. Still, by 1870, the local paper reported that 250 men were employed in the fishery trade. The coming of the railroad brought with it the hope of new markets and a new wave of fishermen, many of them Scandinavian immigrants. By 1885, there were at least 15 sets strung along the mainland from Sand River to Bark Point. Otter Island, Manitou, Stockton, Oak, and others all had net buoys dotting their waters. In 1886, Bayfield fisheries shipped 310,000 pounds of whitefish and 200,000 pounds of lake trout. Fishing had become the new king.

By the time the *Donna Belle* clears the West Channel and turns east into the passage between

Stockton and Hermit Islands, the first brushstrokes of sunrise are painting her wooden sides with orange light. In the growing daylight, I take in the look of the old tug. She is a working vessel—all tar paper, peeled paint, and gull droppings. The hold is strewn with miles of yellow line, a maze of nets, and stacks of grey fish boxes. A collection of orange slickers sways from pegs on the wall. An old jam jar doubles as a light fixture. In the middle of it all, Marty's legs dangle down from the tiny wheelhouse as he steers us toward the nets somewhere northeast of Stockton Island.

With the boom in the industry, fish camps sprang up on many of the islands. There were camps on Rocky and South Twin as early as 1870s. Booth Fisheries ran tugs off Rocky Island for years, starting in 1888, supplying the growing local resort trade as well as packing and shipping Apostle Island lake trout and whitefish to markets as distant as St. Paul, Milwaukee, and Chicago.

At first most commercial fishing was done with gill nets, long strings of nearly invisible netting strung out at different depths and varying locations, depending upon the time of year. The process was simple—schools of fish would swim into the invisible nets. The smaller, noncommercial-sized fish swam right through, while the 4- to 5-inch mesh snagged the larger fish by the gills. Each boat laid strings of nets called "gangs" at several locations around the islands, but since fish caught in gill nets are not kept alive, gangs had to be checked frequently to keep the fish fresh, limiting the number of nets a single boat could manage.

Above: Dave Anderson begins to pull nets aboard *Donna Belle*.
Left: John Hagen, a Madeline Island fisherman, winds a net onto a drying rack, in a photo taken around 1950.
Opposite: Commercial fishing off the *Danny-Boy*.
Inset: Keeping an eye on the weather from inside a fishing tug.

75

Above: Marty Erickson works his nets. He is uncertain how much longer he'll remain a fisherman. Above, right: In a 1930s photograph, local fishermen are lifting their pound nets. Chequamegon Point light on Long Island is visible in the background.

Later many of the operations switched to pound (pronounced "pond") nets. Pound nets were intricate, maze-like net structures mounted on poles that were driven into the lakebed. They were strung in such a way as to funnel fish into a holding area or "pot," where they would be trapped alive and kept fresh until the fishermen could lift the nets. Recently, troubles with cormorants raiding the pound nets and the risk of increasing recreational boat traffic tangling the nets have led many, like Marty Erickson, to go back to fishing with gill nets.

Drying, mending, and setting nets, carving buoys, pounding sinkers, cleaning, packing and transporting fish, maintaining boats, a fish camp was a place that buzzed with hard work. Julian Nelson remembers. Nelson, a long-time Bayfield commercial fisherman, recalls being put to work early by his father, a Norwegian immigrant who had a fish camp on Stockton Island beginning in 1919.

"You need your feet underneath you when you mend nets so you can move around, and I remember I was so little when I started that my Dad had to cut the legs off a chair so my feet could touch the ground."

Nelson, who bought his father out in 1938 and continued fishing for almost fifty years, has a boatload of memories from life at Apostle Islands' fish camps: work, work, and more work. But there are other moments, too, that drift in the fisherman's memory: his father rowing him out to Lone Rock (now called Balancing Rock) on a Saturday evening sight-seeing voyage; swimming among the wreckage of the *Noque Bay*, a lumber boat that burned just offshore; fish tugs like the *C.W. Turner* rounding the point; and big storms that kept them pinned down for days. "The lake is the boss," Nelson says with an authority born of years on the water. "The lake is the boss." He even remembers the day Carl

Ludwigson hired a man to saw a building in half.

"My father and Ludwigson fished together for years off Stockton Island, from about 1920 to the early 30s," Nelson recalls. But something happened between the two and Ludwigson struck out on his own, moving his operation around Anderson Point to a spot near where the National Park Service dock is today. They decided to divide everything equally between them. Nelson chuckles at the memory. "I mean everything." One day after the split, a man showed up with a saw at the small fish shed the two had shared. "I remember the day and I remember the man," Nelson says. "He just climbed right up on the roof and started sawing—sawed that shed right square in half so that Ludwigson could take his half with him."

It wouldn't be the first or the last fishing shack relocated in the Apostles. As neighbors feuded or fishing declined in one area, families simply picked up and moved to another. When a new owner purchased South Twin Island in 1931, raising the "rent" on the fishing shacks there, many picked up their buildings and slid them across the ice to Rocky Island. Julian Nelson himself moved his fishing camp in 1947, floating it by barge from Stockton to Rocky for its safer harbor.

Left: Julian Nelson has lived in the Apostles Islands all of his life, where he fished from the time he was a boy working with his father. Below: Gilmore Young, once Julian Nelson's fishing partner, photographed as he maintained the nets at camp on Stockton Island in the early 40s.

Without warning, the *Donna Belle* throttles back. Marty Erickson maneuvers close to a black-and-white buoy, bolts out of the pilot house, snags the buoy with a hook, and pulls the leading edge of his first set in through a large hatch on the starboard side. Erickson, who has worked on fishing boats since he was in sixth grade, moves with a practiced precision. Every move is efficient and confident, honed by repetition. Erickson winds the leading edge of the set around the lift wheel and spins it until it catches. Controlling the lift's throttle with one hand and steering the boat with the other by using a system of chains and pulleys, Erickson watches as the turn after turn of the long

Above: Commercial fisherman Joe Duffy, a Red Cliff tribal member, fishes for whitefish and lake trout. Opposite: Gulls crowd around a fishing boat looking for an easy meal.

net is brought in empty. Not a single fish. Then he is into the fish.

For a time it is a frenzy. Four fish, six fish, a dozen, each untangled, gaffed, tossed into a fish box, the net spraying water, the boat rocking, the lift wheel spinning. It is a dance of fish scales, spray, gulls, and waves—a dance that would be instantly recognized by generations of Apostle Islands fishermen.

Island fishing history is today preserved at places like Manitou Island fish camp, now maintained by the National Park Service. The ramshackle collection of weathered, gray buildings with gossamer strings of old nets, a home-made boat winch, hatchet-carved wooden buoys, and improvised, nail-studded ice shoes was once a poor man's fishing camp. It was a place where local men—mostly bachelors—could wait out bleak times while yanking a modest living from Lake Superior with just a hand jig, an ice pick, and a lot of patience. For decades, beginning in the early 1900s the camp hosted a string of colorful characters—men with names like "Jinglin' Johnson," "Black Pete," and Hjalmer "Governor" Olson. The men mainly fished here in winter, setting their nets beneath the ice, then muscling their modest catch the three miles across the ice to the mainland on wooden sleds. The sleds were usually pulled by sheer will, but occasionally with the help of a horse named Jim and once with a Model A that ran a few trips between Manitou and Ironwood Island until a snowstorm brought it to a halt.

The Hokenson Fishery at Little Sand Bay on the mainland, also maintained by the National Park Service, is an example of the more substantial fishing operations that once dotted the lakeshore. Starting with just three nets and one small boat in 1927, the Hokenson brothers—Leo, Eskel, and Roy—began fishing only, as Florence Hokenson once said, because "farming wasn't going too well . . . we could hold up a mirror and watch ourselves starve to

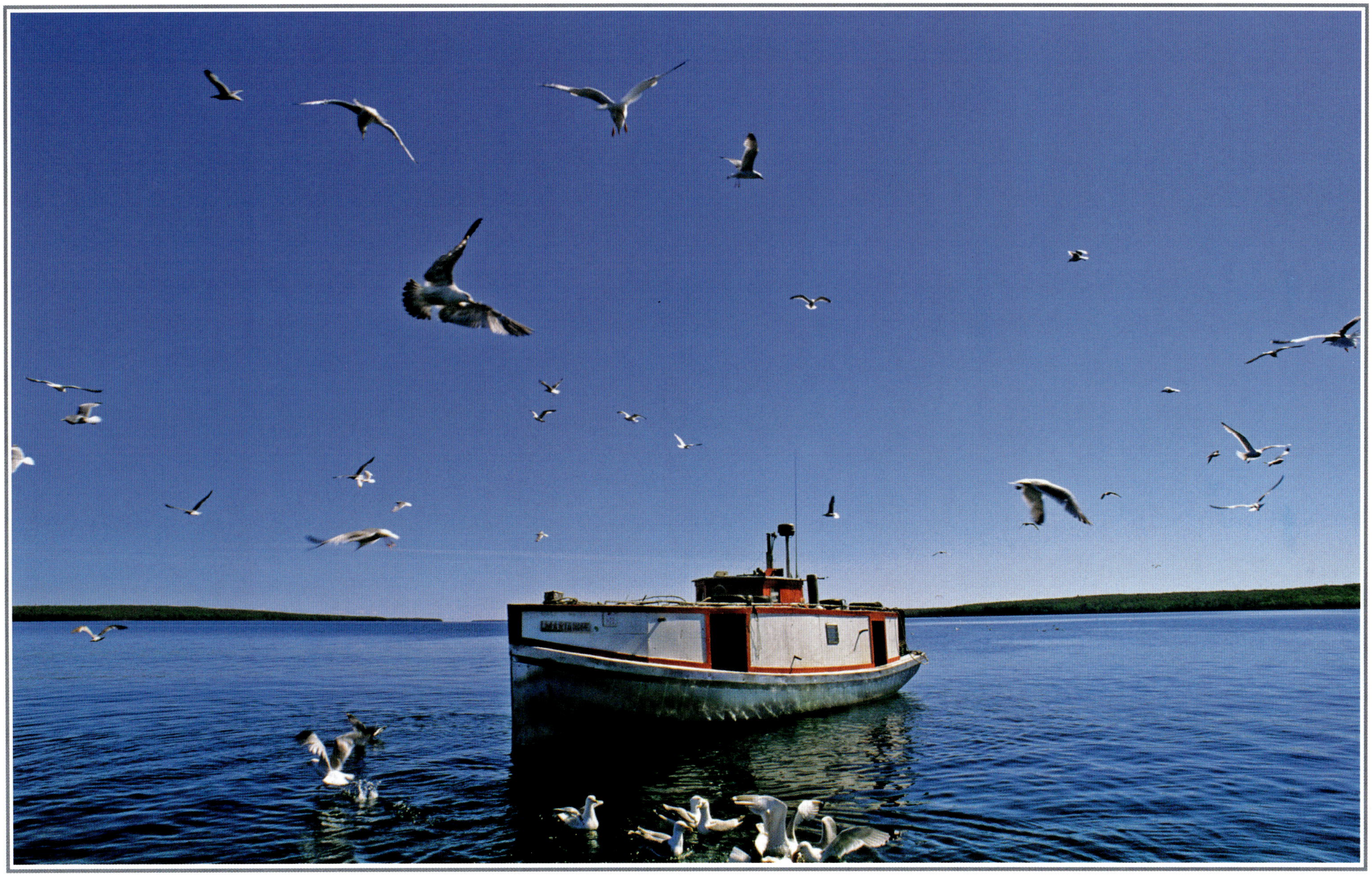

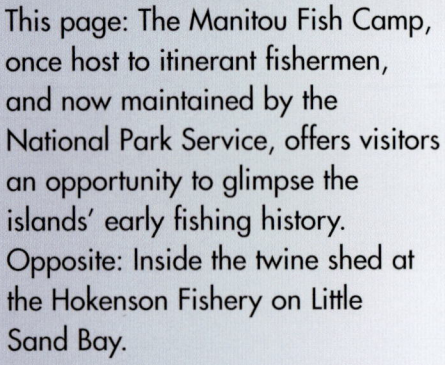

This page: The Manitou Fish Camp, once host to itinerant fishermen, and now maintained by the National Park Service, offers visitors an opportunity to glimpse the islands' early fishing history. Opposite: Inside the twine shed at the Hokenson Fishery on Little Sand Bay.

death." Still, they built the operation with skill and determination, watching it grow through the years to include as many as 15 nets, a 38-foot fishing tug called the *Twilite*, and a compound that boasted a twine shed, an ice house, a substantial dock and herring shed, and a fine home overlooking the lake. They did it by focusing on the "money fish," lake trout and whitefish, and corralling great swarms of them into their pound nets.

The 1940s and 50s were the heyday of commercial fishing. Catches of lake trout in the Wisconsin waters of Lake Superior soared to 291 tons, up 100 tons from the averages in the decades just before that. Herring too seemed to flow into the nets in prodigious numbers. In a frenzied three-week burst in November, fishermen would battle the growing cold and rough seas to bring in almost unfathomable catches of herring—some 2,700 tons a year from Wisconsin waters of the big lake.

Julian Nelson remembers. On his boats the *Beth Suzanne* and later the *Mermaid*, Nelson recalls netting 100 tons of herring in a season—as many as nine tons in a single day. "It was a bonanza, in terms of money," he says, "but an incredible amount of work, too. Every one of those nine tons of fish had to be hand-picked out of the net and cleaned. They average three to the pound, so you do the math."

Despite the work, there must have been a magic to herring season—the docks noisy with the clamor of workers unloading, cleaning, and packing fish, and the rumble of loaded barrels rolling up and down the dock. At the Hokenson Fishery, everyone helped at herring time—wives, children, friends, and hired hands. "Those were the days," Julian Nelson says wistfully. "But catches like those were once-in-a-lifetime. You won't see those again." And perhaps he is right.

Erickson pulls aboard the end of the net, an orange-flagged buoy weighted with a brick. He cleans off some strands of lake grass and steps quickly to the open stern, tossing the leading edge off the back, to start the process of re-setting the net. Fewer than two dozen lake trout flop in the fish boxes. A combination of over-fishing and the infestation of the parasitic sea lamprey sent the catches plummeting, as early as the mid-1950s. Once Lake Superior as a whole netted 4.5 million pounds of lake trout a year. By 1960 that figure dropped to less than a half million. Among the Apostles, many nets grew light.

Increased regulation, stagnant market prices, and a buy-out plan for commercial fishing licenses have further chipped away at the industry, until fewer than a dozen commercial fishing boats operate among the islands today. Erickson, a fourth-generation Apostle Islands fisherman whose great-grandfather first lifted nets here in 1905, isn't sure the

Above: Bill "Binks" Gordon is a retired Ojibwe fisherman from Red Cliff.
Opposite: Marty Erickson heads out at 4:00 am aboard *Donna Belle* to check his nets.

Donna Belle will be among them for much longer.

"Work's hard, but the pay is bad," Erickson says with a smile as tosses out the anchor buoy and steers the boat toward the next set. He's seen catches of up to 1,000 pounds in a single run, though he says "I've seen more than my share of 100-pound days, too." On this day Erickson will lift two gangs, six separate nets, and turn back for Bayfield with just 450 pounds of fish on ice. At the current market price of 30 cents a pound, the day's catch will net him $135, hardly enough to cover fuel, ice, equipment, and other expenses.

But the job does have its benefits. "No one to tell you what to do or how to do it, lunch on the deck, and I've got a pretty good view from my office," Erickson says with the boat on autopilot as we grab a bite to eat in the sun between sets. The islands pass by in a long parade of green shorelines framed with blue sky and blue lake, shorelines that have seen generations of fish camps and fishermen. As we pass Rocky Island, someone waves from a dock.

These islands would not be the same without the slow thrum of the fishing tugs plowing their way through the channels. Still, a man and his family cannot survive on sunshine. You can't put a nice view in the bank. Erickson says the *Donna Belle* needs $12,000 to $15,000 worth of repairs this winter, and he admits he is considering another occupation, perhaps welding. When I ask him if he'll still be fishing in ten years, he doesn't think long. "I sure hope not," he says. "I am not even sure I'll be doing it next year. It's year-to-year, day-to-day in this business."

In the silence that follows, another fishing boat appears far off, lifting its own set, a cloud of gulls drifting lazily behind. It is a simple sight that speaks of backbreaking work, high waves, and history, a sight whose days may be numbered among the islands. With the nets picked clean and reset, the boat turns its course and vanishes into the haze. I can't help wondering, as we chug toward the next set, if the *Donna Belle* and the rest of the Apostle Islands fishing industry won't soon follow, disappearing into the haze of history somewhere over the lake.

↓ 83

Above: Captain John Geisheker instructs Marit Swanson, Jim Schuler (at helm) and Greg Corniea on the fine points of sailing. For students and experienced sailors alike, sailing Lake Superior is a never-ending challenge. Summer brings competition, racing schools, and leisurely cruises to the Apostle Islands.

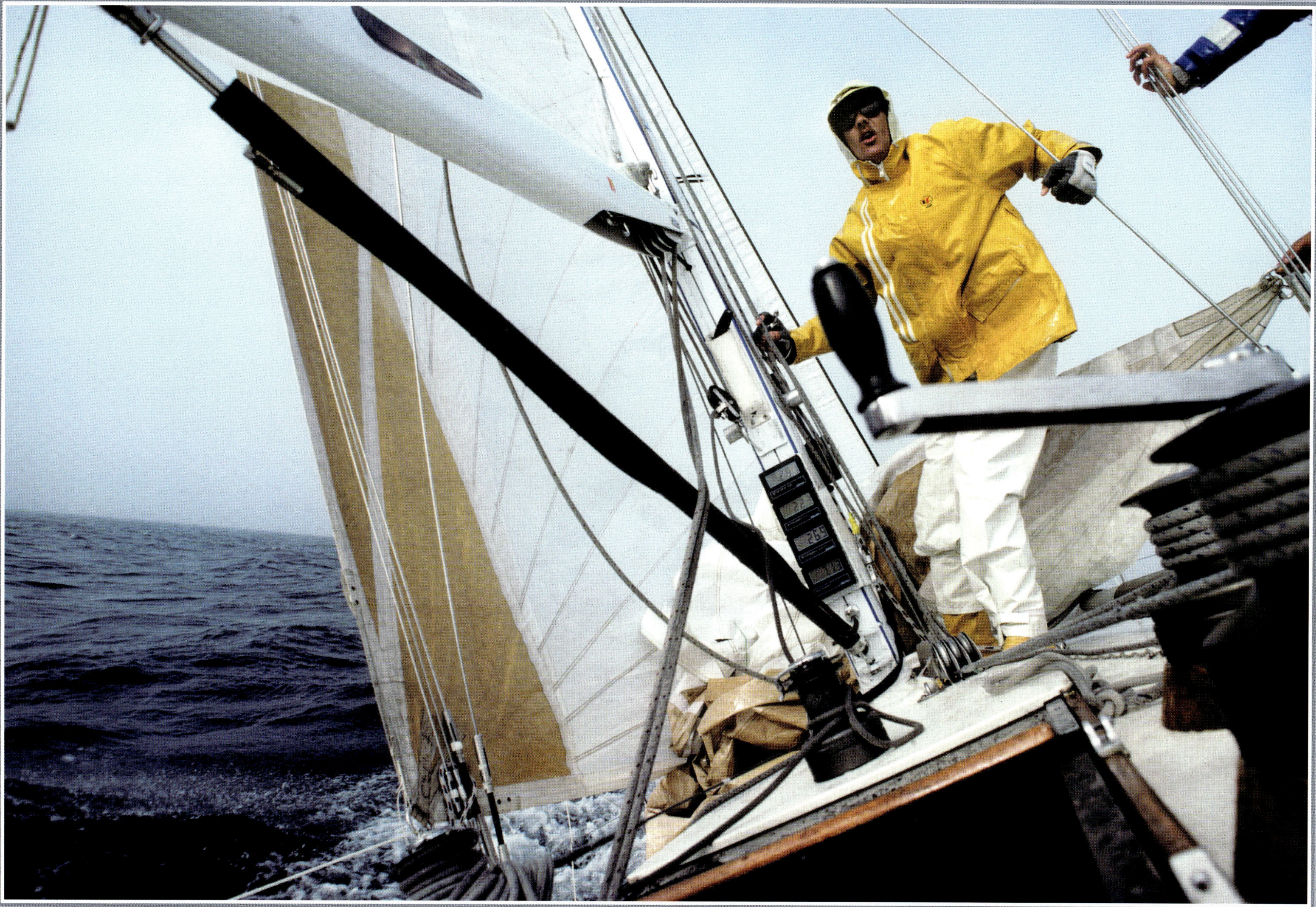

Among the Islands: A Journey with Postcards

There is a sound a sailboat makes—sailors know it—when everything is in perfect trim and exactly right, when the main is taut, the jib is set, and wind fills every square inch of sail. The hull nearly leaps from the water as if about to take flight, the bow slicing the waves with a sound like wings carving the air

That's the sound Captain Mike Radtke is listening for as he stands at the helm of *Reverie*, a 38-foot sloop, calling instructions. "Take the jib in just a bit" he yells. And I do, feeling the muscle of the wind tug the sail taut. *Reverie* jumps to the command, her sails cupping with sweet Superior air.

These islands have long drawn sailors, tourists, adventurers, picnickers, and sightseers. As early as the middle 1850s their faces smile back from glossy Apostle Island postcards—daguerreotype photographs of parasol-toting ladies and men in top hats strolling the docks, or hand-tinted scenes of rowboats and lighthouses, beachcombers in knee-length swim trunks under skies daubed with sunset colors. "Paradise on the Lake," they say over a rowboat at the foot of Honeymoon Rock or "Among the Islands" above lovers stringing a beach with footprints. They are mementoes of summer days, three-by-five cards capturing a moment of island beauty

Even more than nets teeming with lake trout, more than loads of lumber and brownstone, natural beauty has always been the greatest resource of the Apostle Islands. It is a beauty that was recognized early. "The Apostles," author Charles Lanhan wrote in 1848, "consist of three islands [that] stud the waters most charmingly."

The number may be wrong but the feeling is familiar—that glint of sunlight off the water, the reach of the long blue horizon-anchored islands. A travel writer for the *Cincinnati Gazette* recognized it in 1856 when he wrote, "We cannot imagine a more delightful or healthier retreat than these Isles . . . Saratoga, Cape May, and all the fashionable watering places sink to insignificance as locales when compared with the Apostle Islands. The atmosphere is pure and exhilarating."

"Let your imagination picture a handsome little

town nestling 'neath romantic bluffs," the local paper wrote of Bayfield in 1887, "and at its feet the blue waters of the grandest of inland seas, while in the distance like gems of living green, the far famed Apostle Islands."

Many did let their imaginations and more wander to those "far famed" Apostles. As the railroad reached Bayfield in 1883, the tourist business boomed. Trainloads of visitors came to be towed by barge to Madeline Island for Fourth of July celebrations or to watch sailing regattas on the bay. Hay fever sufferers came for the pollen-free lake air; others to dip their toes in the chilly water and beat the city heat. Visitors stayed at the Madeline House on Madeline Island and at Bayfield's luxurious Island View Hotel, with its parquet-floored ballrooms, broad-railed porch, and a "table supplied with everything money and energy can secure." Later, the more adventurous booked rooms at rustic lodges like Camp Stella on Sand Island.

This was an era of grand summer homes. The Allen C. Fuller House (now the Old Rittenhouse Inn) was built in 1890, with 21 rooms and 7 fireplaces as an escape from hay fever for the former Civil War general. The Madeline Island home of Colonel Fredrick Wood of Lincoln, Nebraska (today Wood Manor), was constructed in 1898, and was the first in a string of summer homes that would rise along what is still known today as Nebraska Row.

Whether people came for a weekend or to while away the summer, Bayfield and Madeline Island became the jumping-off points for the Apostle Islands, and the social centers of the northern summering crowd. Music wafted from the opera house that once stood along the shoreline beside the Waiting Pavilion (called the gazebo today) where passengers awaited the departure of excursion boats that took them on tours among the islands. The

Upper left: The Old Rittenhouse Inn is a landmark in Bayfield, known for its gourmet fare and the Victorian-era decor of its dining rooms.
Above: Wood Manor on Madeline Island is now operated as tourist lodging.
Opposite: A wooden sailboat docked at Bayfield casts its reflection in the bay.
Inset: The bow of a powerboat nosing toward Basswood Island.

Above: President Calvin Coolidge and his wife caused a local stir when they toured aboard the yacht *Nellewood* in 1928.

Opposite, top: Sportfishing is one of many activities that may be pursued near the Apostle Islands.

Lower: Marinas at Bayfield, Red Cliff, LaPointe, Washburn and Ashland are home to a variety of boats that sail or motor here.

area's growing popularity with tourists led to calls for its protection. As early as 1891, the local paper proposed the creation of an Apostle Islands National Park, but support for the idea grew slowly—too slowly, as it turned out. Hidden beneath the soft waves of dance music and laughter of the summer crowd was the endless hum of the buzz saws. The same islands that drew the tourists with their beauty were being logged mercilessly while the summer crowd danced.

A visit by President Calvin Coolidge in 1928, which included a lunch of local lake trout on the rocky shelf of Devils Island, renewed interest and hope in the park idea. Finally in 1929 supporters of the park initiative, led by H.H. Peavey, a Wisconsin congressmen from Washburn, persuaded the Department of Interior to commission a study of the potential park. By then, however, it was nearly too late.

In August of 1930 Harlan Kelsey, a consultant for the National Park Service, toured the area. He was taken to the top of Ole Olson Hill on the mainland for the view, given an aerial look at the islands by plane, and was boated among them aboard the 96-foot *Lemora*, a Madeline Island yacht. Kelsey's initial reaction, given in speeches he made locally following the tour, raised hopes among supporters; but his official report, issued six months later, dashed them again.

"What must have been once a far more striking and characteristic landscape of dark coniferous forest has been obliterated by the ax followed by fire," Kelsey wrote in the January 1931 report. "The virgin forests have been ruthlessly exterminated mostly within the last 5-20 years . . . The ecological conditions have been so violently disturbed that probably never can they be more than remotely reproduced." Not surprisingly, his report did not recommend including the Apostle Islands alongside Yellowstone, Yosemite, the Grand Canyon, and other gems of the national park system. Instead it warned that if present practices continued, places like Outer Island would end up a "smoldering desolate waste."

A second survey of the area a year later, conducted this time by Arno Cammerer, the Associate Director of the National Park Service, came to much the same conclusion. "The cut-over character of the land was an insurmountable obstacle to its being considered a national park." Still, the more diplomatic and visionary Cammerer did offer at least a glimmer of hope. "This area," he wrote after his tour here, "holds marvelous recreational opportunities for the future, and in time, will come into its own." Arno Cammerer himself could not have imagined just how prophetic those words would turn out to be.

"Right there," Captain Radtke calls from the helm as I haul in the jib. "Cleat it off." And I do. All around us the air hums with sound—the hull slashing through the waves, the lines taut as harp strings, the wind singing in the canvas—the sounds of perfect sailing. For three days Mike and I, along with our families, will sail among the Apostles with no itinerary and no plan, just a good ship, a good breeze, and time.

It takes time to really see these islands, to really see them. As beautiful as they are, the Apostles are a difficult place to come to know. There is no one place, no lookout, on land or water where all the islands are visible at once. They can't be taken in that easily. Even if there were such a place, even if you could glimpse it all with a single turn of the head, one view is never the whole story. Sands shift in a storm, uncovering a shipwreck; flocks of birds descend silently in a bog at dusk and rise again at dawn, their wings barely stirring the morning air.

This is a place that reveals its secrets slowly. Here, you collect memories in pieces, over a summer, over a string of summers, over a lifetime. The only way to come to know these islands is to return again and again, year after year, season after season, collecting images like

89

> Honeymoon Rock, Basswood Island
> February
> CRACK! Twenty below, and the ice is groaning where I am camped alone on the north side of Basswood Island. The ice is cracking and the lights are out—northern lights, curtains of green tinged with spikes of orange like flames, so close it seems as if I could stir the colors with the tips of my fingers. They flicker to every horizon as I walk away from my tent, reflecting on the ice, the light overhead dancing in unison with its reflection below. Alone, far off of Honeymoon Rock, I lie on the ice, peering straight up into the lights. It is, I think to myself, like being inside of a diamond. I watch until the cold seeps into my bones and I shiver—whether from the cold or from the sheer beauty of the sky above me, I cannot exactly say.

falling leaves, like colorful pebbles on a beach, like postcards.

With the sails tightly trimmed, and *Reverie* set on its course, I work my way forward to sit with my legs dangling over the side. I think about time, about the islands, about those old postcards. With each island that ticks by, I write my own postcards to myself, memories from my own fifteen years among the Apostle Islands.

With *Reverie* making a steady eight knots, we string the islands like beads on the white thread of our wake—Stockton, Ironwood. Then, somewhere between North Twin and Outer Island, things begin to change. The wind freshens, gusting to 24 knots, making the boat heel just far enough to give you that dull ache in the pit of your stomach. Below, the

> Hole-in-the-Wall, Oak Island, July
> We slide past Hole-in-the-Wall, where a reach of ancient sandstone wraps its brown arm around a chip of blue sky. The sight always reminds me of pirates and a story. An island legend says that a group of pirates, the 12 Apostles, hid somewhere near here in the 1800s, using the wilds of Oak Island as a base from which to rob passing ships. They would set out in the fog, paddling silently up to ships to raid them, returning here with their loot. It is a story often told at bedtime to children who love these islands, and ever since we have had to stop here any time we went boating by, to walk the beach and look for peg-legged prints in the sand.

⚓ 91

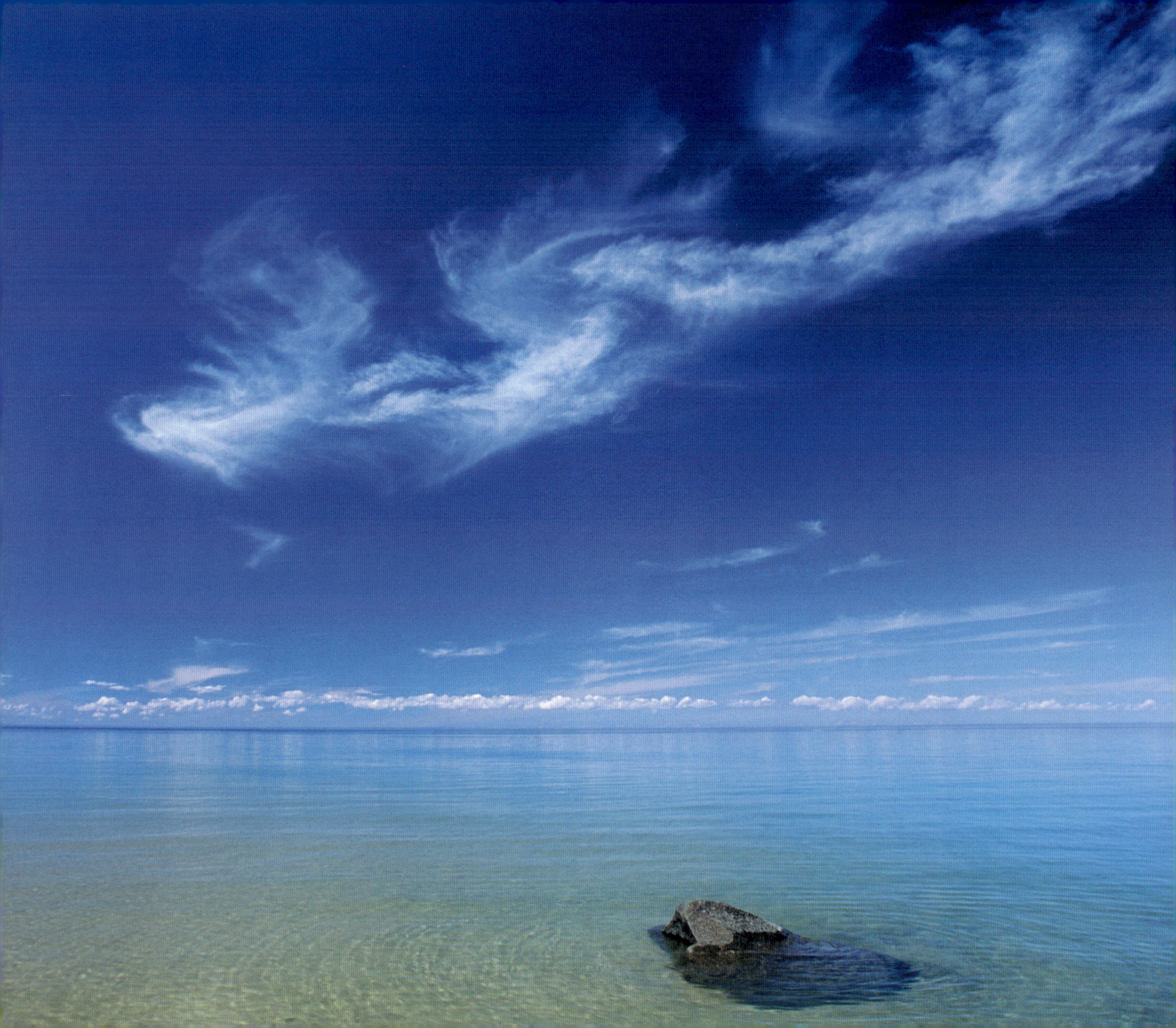

kids scream excitedly, cheering each big wave. The lake has grown darker, rippled blue to black, and clouds the color of gray steel hang like curtains on the horizon.

It is another world this far out in the Apostles. As you clear the northern tip of Outer Island, the horizons open, blue-winged and endless. The wind and the waves, untethered across three hundred miles of open lake, grow bigger and stronger and wilder. The secure feeling of the inner islands and bays is lost. As we reach our furthest point from land, I write another postcard.

> Outer Island
> With a 24-knot wind off our port bow, we glide past the safe reach of the island's arms and into the big blue heart of the lake, just for a taste of its power. Lake Superior is a lake so huge its outline is visible from the moon, so vast it takes the sunrise half an hour to cross its face. We sail straight on until Outer Island grows charcoal gray, hazy with distance, and we are swallowed by hues of blue—the dark blue of the deep water, the hazy blue of the distance, the softer blue of the sky. A lake, said Henry David Thoreau, is "the grandest expression of the landscape, the Earth's eye." On this day, in this light, Superior is a shining eye of blue.

"Coming about," Mike calls from the helm. We curl a long, graceful turn away from the open horizons and back to the safe confines of the islands.

With a splash we drop the hook in a protected bay off Cat Island, where we will spend the night, rowing to landfall at sunset to walk the comma-shaped beach along the island's northeastern shore. A flock of gulls rises like spindrift as the kids run ahead in the sand.

Cat Island, like most of the Apostles, was heavily logged. But walk the beach at Cat Island today and it is difficult to imagine the "smoldering desolate" wasteland of those days. Time has been at work here, and among all the islands. After the failed national park push of the 1930s the Great Depression altered the economics of island

Above: Swimming in Lake Superior is, at best, *brief*. Even in summer, the water remains frigid enough to induce hypothermia, warming only slightly in protected bays.
Opposite: A meditative view off York Island reveals the stunning clarity of Lake Superior water.

⚓ 93

resources. Logging slowed. Farmers and settlers left the islands to look for other work, and the land reverted to the state for taxes. The islands were forgotten.

And something interesting happened. Slowly, a second-growth forest began to spring up in the clear-cuts. Wildflowers softened the sharp angles of the brownstone quarries. Saplings tested the edges of cleared fields. Left alone, the islands experienced a kind of ecological renewal, a "re-wilding," as author James Feldman has called it. The ecosystem that would spring up in the wake of the heavy logging and fires and quarrying was different from what had once cloaked the islands. It had to be. The ecological footprint of the Apostles had been changed. But the words of Arno Cammerer so long ago began to ring true. These islands did hold "marvelous recreational opportunities for the future." Given time they have indeed "come into [their] own."

Slowly the charm of the "far famed Apostles" seeped back in, and the world took notice. In the 1940s a photographer from the prestigious magazine *Life* chose York Island to take photographs for a piece on "the best sunsets in the United States." By 1959, Oak and Stockton Islands had recovered enough to be made part of the state forest system. The 1960s brought a Boy Scout Jamboree to Otter Island and, perhaps more importantly, the 60s brought the dawn of the environmental movement. As thoughts turned to the plight of the planet, the prospects of a national park in the Apostle Islands were rekindled from the ashes of the earlier attempts, and the idea found a new and powerful champion—Gaylord Nelson.

"There is not another collection of islands of this significance within the continental boundaries of the United States," Nelson wrote. "I think it is tremendously important that this collection of islands be preserved." First as Wisconsin governor from 1958 to 1962 and later in the U.S. Senate, Nelson took every opportunity to sing the praises of the Apostle Islands. The idea received strong support from conservationist and author Sigurd Olson, who urged that this "superb string of islands be immediately designated . . . as a unit of the National Wilderness Preservation System." But the most powerful voice was yet to be heard.

There was concern in Washington that the Apostles still did not rise to a level of grandeur that would allow them to stand beside the gems of the national park system. But the growing nation was looking for recreational opportunities closer to home. In 1963, the Presidential Recreation Advisory Council proposed a system of national recreation areas. The areas to be given protection under this new category, the Council concluded, would need to include at least 20,000 acres of land and water, would sit within 250 miles of urban population centers, and would possess natural endowments "well above the ordinary in quality and recreational appeal." The very definition seemed to point directly at the Apostle Islands, and the president himself was about to see it firsthand.

In September of 1963, President John F. Kennedy visited the area. As his helicopter swung out over the Apostle Islands, the President glanced out of the window with mild interest at the splash of the green islands in the blue of the lake. And then he saw the sailboats.

Above: Sailboats at anchor off the Raspberry Island sandspit.
Opposite: An aerial view taking in several of the islands.

Above: The beach at Julian Bay on Stockton Island is a long stretch of fine, smooth sand—sometimes referred to as the "singing sands." Inset: Ripe blueberries, found midsummer in patches throughout the islands, are greatly prized once sampled.

As a sailor himself, the President immediately saw the potential of the Apostle Islands spelled out in the multi-colored sails curling among the islands. By the time he reached the podium set up for him at the Ashland airport, he was convinced. "Anyone who flies over those islands as we just did," President Kennedy said that day, "looks at that long beach, looks at those marshes, sees what a tremendous natural resource this can be."

It would take another seven years, seemingly endless public meetings, and countless adjustments in the proposed boundaries, but on September 26, 1970, President Richard Nixon signed Public Law 91-424 conserving for "the benefit, inspiration, education, recreational use, and enjoyment of the public" 20 of the 22 Apostle Islands (Long Island was added in 1986) and a 12-mile stretch of the mainland shore. The Apostle Islands National Lakeshore was born.

After a breakfast of pancakes dotted with islands of blueberries, we pull the anchors out of the sand and slip *Reverie* out of the bay. For two more days we'll sail among the islands, part of the 200,000 people a year who now visit the Apostle Islands National Lakeshore. We'll walk the sand spit on Rocky Island searching for flicker feathers, and drift in mid-channel between Ironwood and Otter Island, as the kids cannonball off the swim deck into the jade green water. We'll move with the winds, losing all track of time. Time moves differently among the islands, as if the hours themselves were walking barefoot in the sand.

In those drifting hours I'll think again of postcards, the old ones and my own. Though we tend to look at places like the Apostles as pretty picture postcards, the islands are not stuck in time. They change with every wave. Every wind can blow a new seed to germinate or carry a new species of bird to an island. Every burst of sunlight fuels the growth and re-growth of the forest. Every soft rain brings new life.

If the islands teach us anything, it is that nature never stands still. Time has been at work in these islands. That a place can look and feel this wild, only decades after having been so heavily changed by the hand of man, is a testament to the resiliency of nature. It should give us hope that humans and nature can coexist, as they do here in the Apostle Islands National Lakeshore.

Finally, late on the last afternoon of our trip, we turn back for Bayfield, running wing and wing, the main and the jib eased out on opposite sides to capture the wind straight at our backs. With the sun warm on my face, I write a final postcard.

> Among the Apostles
> Heading for home
> Turning back towards port now, the wind is perfect. Full-sailed and steady we string the islands together like beads on the necklace of our wake — Bear Island, Otter Island, Ironwood and Cat. Each one appears in the distance, draws near, and slips behind, full of stories, full of silence, protected now for all of us: Outer Island, Michigan, Manitou, and Oak, islands of beauty, islands of history, islands of hope.

Above: A place where the aims of an earlier era carry through to today: a desire to live close to Lake Superior, expressed in houses along the shore at La Pointe.

Forever Wild

The rasp of the logger's saw has quieted. In the quarries the blast of the steam hammers has gone still. The days when lumber and stone were king have slipped away among these islands. Now deer browse and wildflowers grow where there were once farm fields and fish camps. Eagles nest in trees spared from the buzz saws. And like water surging in behind a handful of sand cupped from a beach at the wave-like, wildness has flowed back in to the Apostle Islands.

Here that wildness is not the howling, head-spinning, make-you-weak-in-the-knees kind of wilderness found in some national parks. There are no sky-high waterfalls or bottomless canyons, no row-upon-row of snow-capped peaks outreaching every horizon. But after decades of protection, a kind natural rhythm has returned. It is a wildness found in the small things – the rasp of storm waves on a beach, a skein of shorebirds moving low along the water, the slow groan of ice or the sparkle of northern lights. It is embroidered in bear tracks, in the rumor of wolves, and the ancient music of a bog. It is the bass drum of waves pounding the shore at Outer Island and in the quiet drip of a spring sun melting a winter's ice in the Devils Island sea caves. It is sometimes a feeling more than anything you can name or pinpoint on a map.

But on December 8, 2004, that feeling became official. On that day President George W. Bush signed into law a bill passed by Congress creating the Gaylord A. Nelson National Wilderness. With the signing, some 80 percent of the land within the Apostle Islands National Lakeshore (excluding Basswood, Long, and Sand Islands, as well as the mainland section) became a part of the National Wilderness Preservation System linking the Apostles with such famous wild places as Alaska's Denali National Park, the Boundary Waters Canoe Area in Minnesota, and Michigan's Isle Royale National Park.

Created to "secure for this and future generations an enduring resource of wilderness," the National Wilderness Preservation System designation ensures that never again will the Apostle Islands be commercially logged or farmed. There will be no roads, no motorized recreation on the islands, no mining or development. This place, the law says, will stay forever wild.

"The new designation is official recognition of how important a resource these islands really are," says Park Superintendent Bob Krumenaker. "Most of the Apostles are now a wilderness area, as well as a part of the national park system – there is no higher protection. It's the crowning glory of those who fought so long to protect them."

Stand along the shore on one of these islands and you can almost hear the stories of loggers and farmers in the wind through the white pines and the voices of the keepers and fishermen in the waves. That will not change. With this new designation power boaters will still tie up to the docks. Hikers will still climb the winding staircases of the lighthouses and campers will still gather around the campfires to watch the island sunsets. The creation of the Gaylord Nelson Wilderness simply ensures that things will stay that way. It is recognition of the value, not in lumber or stone, but in the existence of a place where natural forces prevail. Here in these islands, these "gems of living green," the new law says, nature that will prevail, forever.

⚓ 99

100

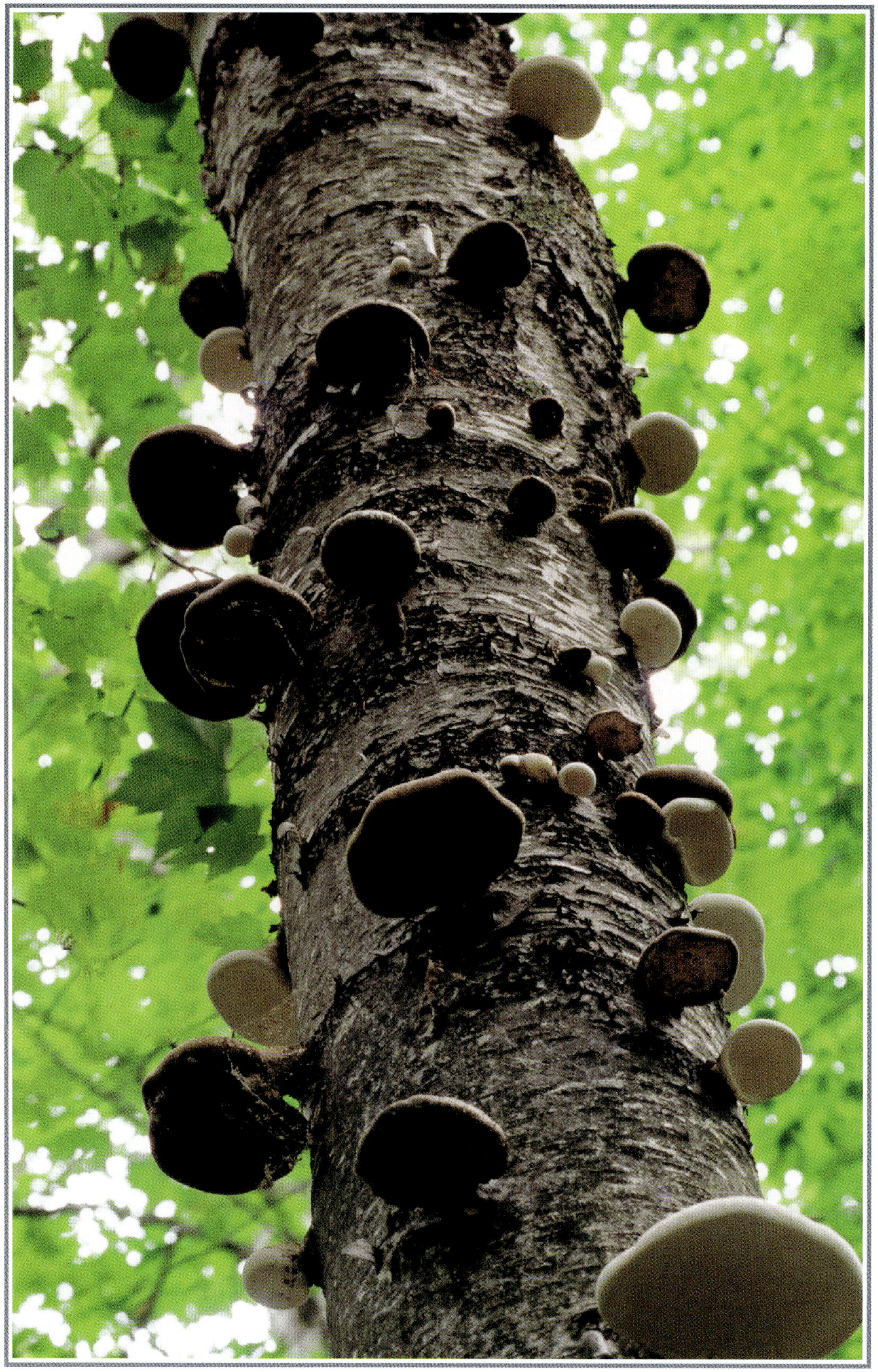
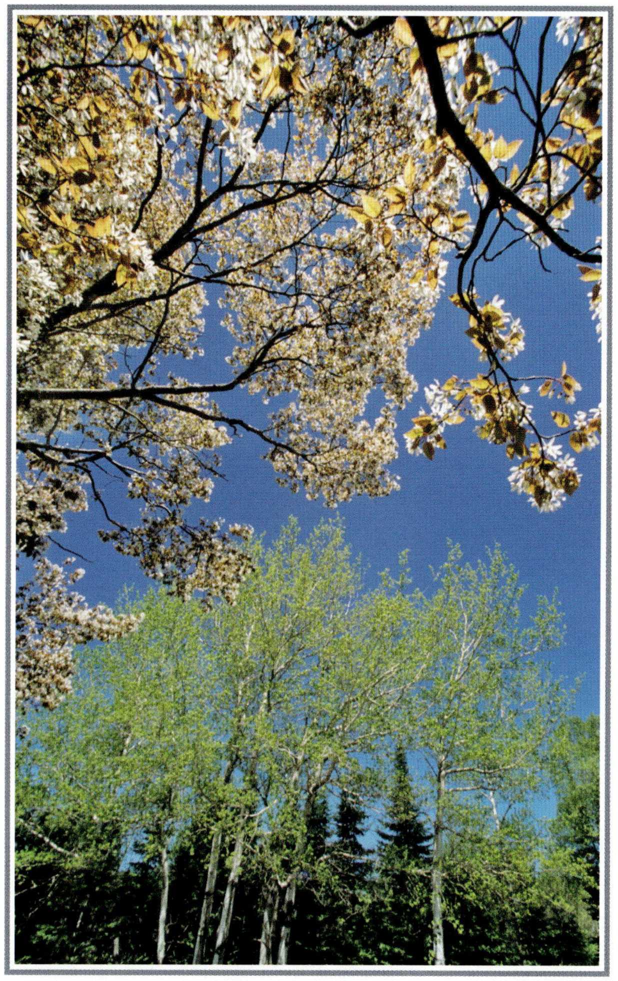
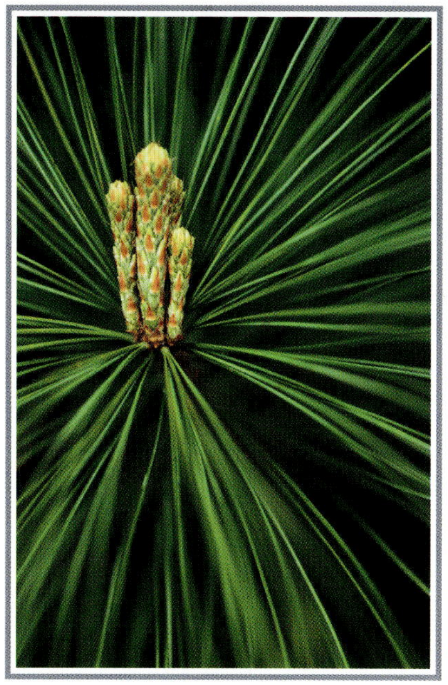
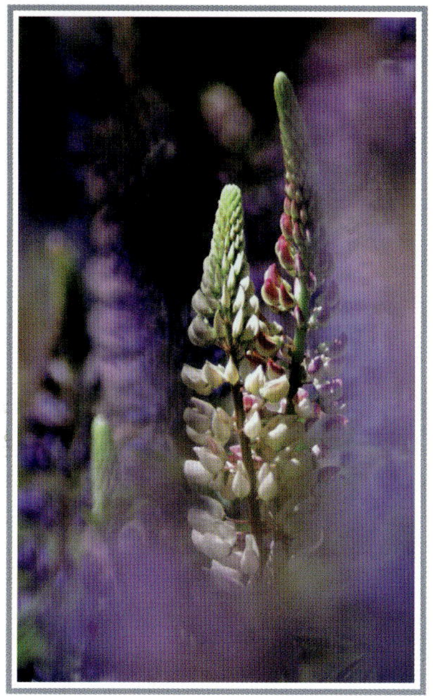

102

103

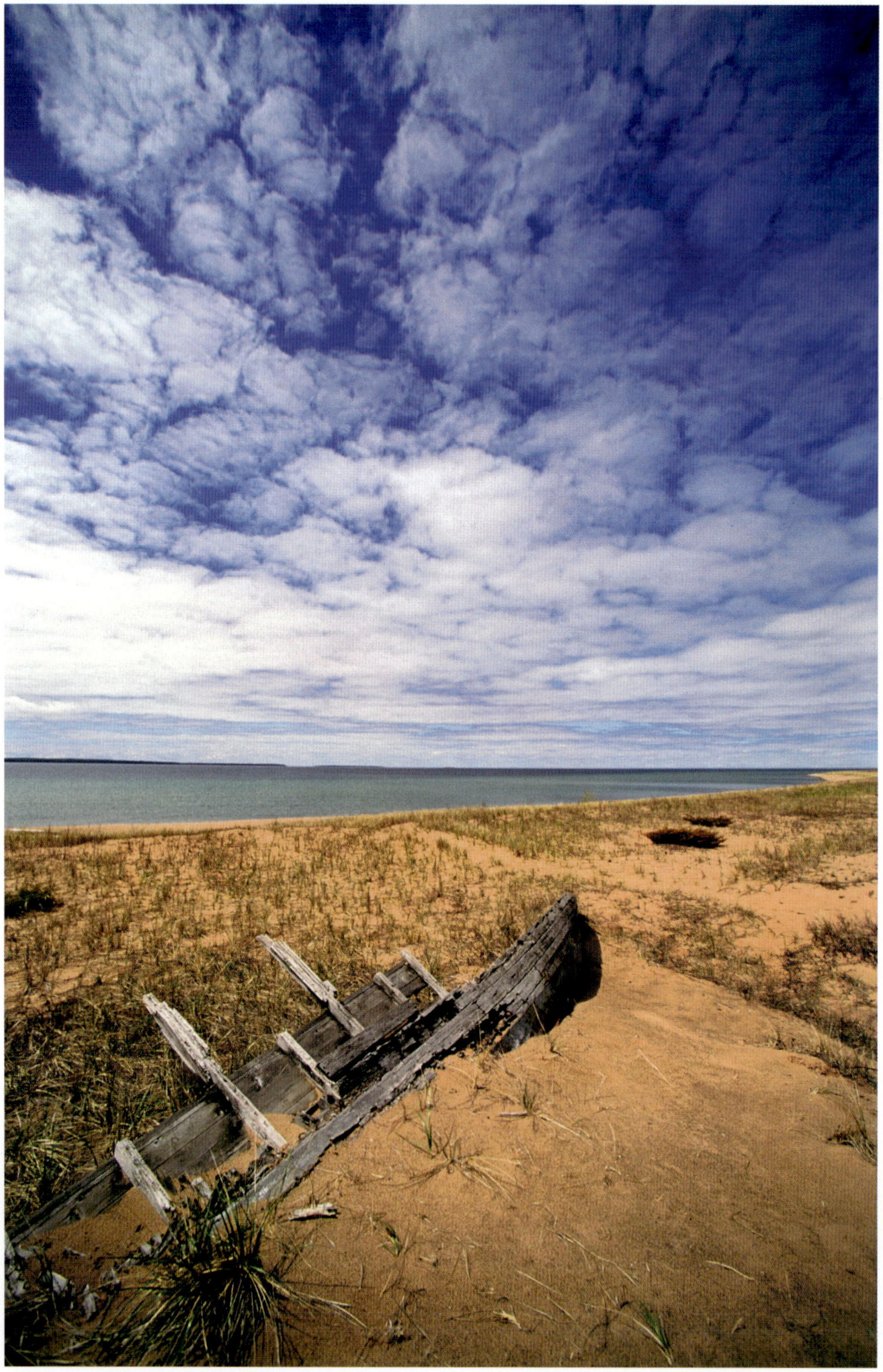

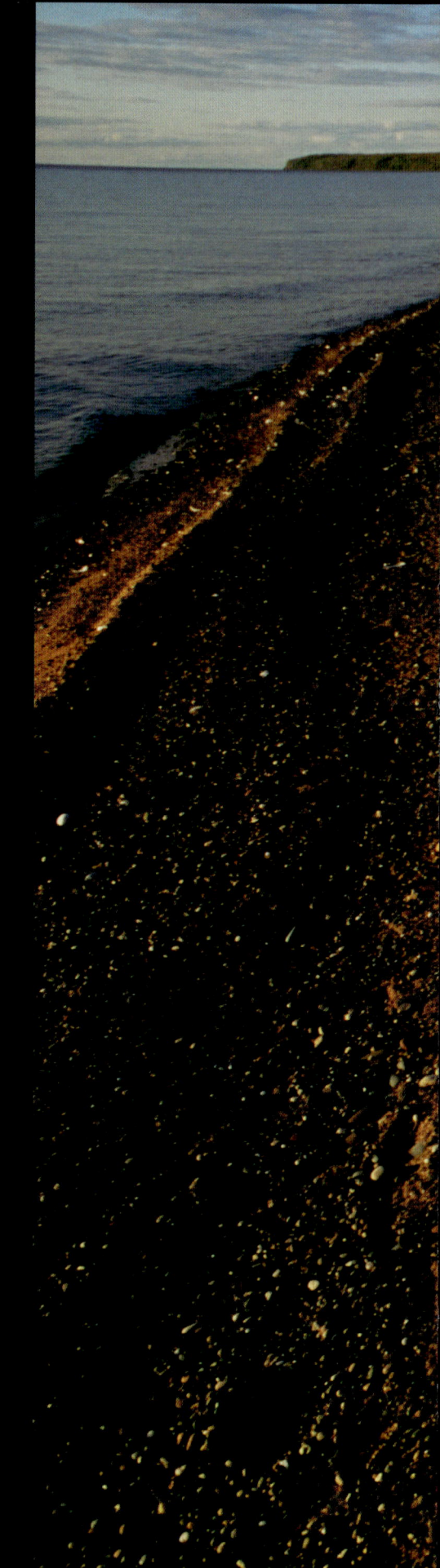

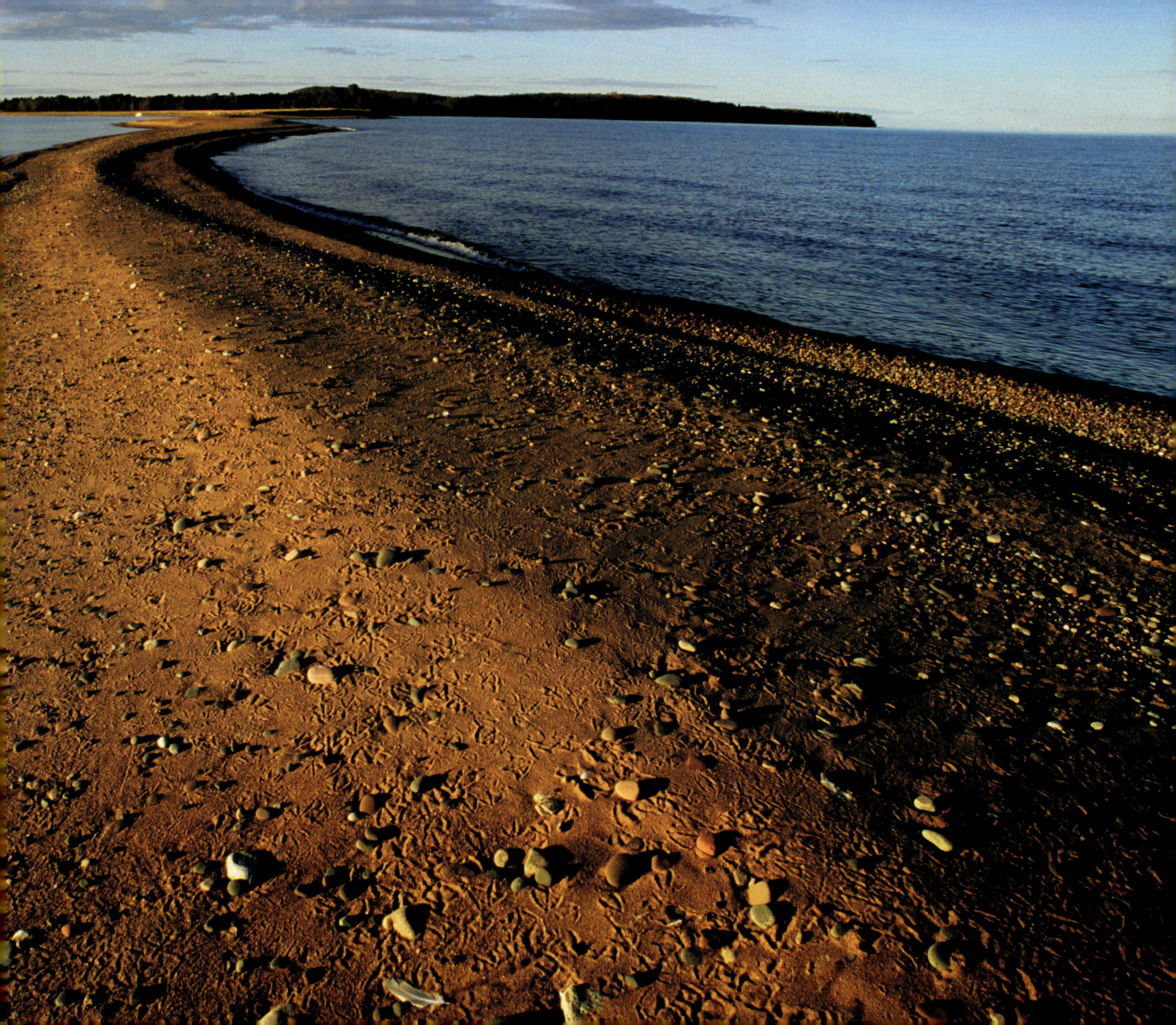

106

107

108

⚓ 109

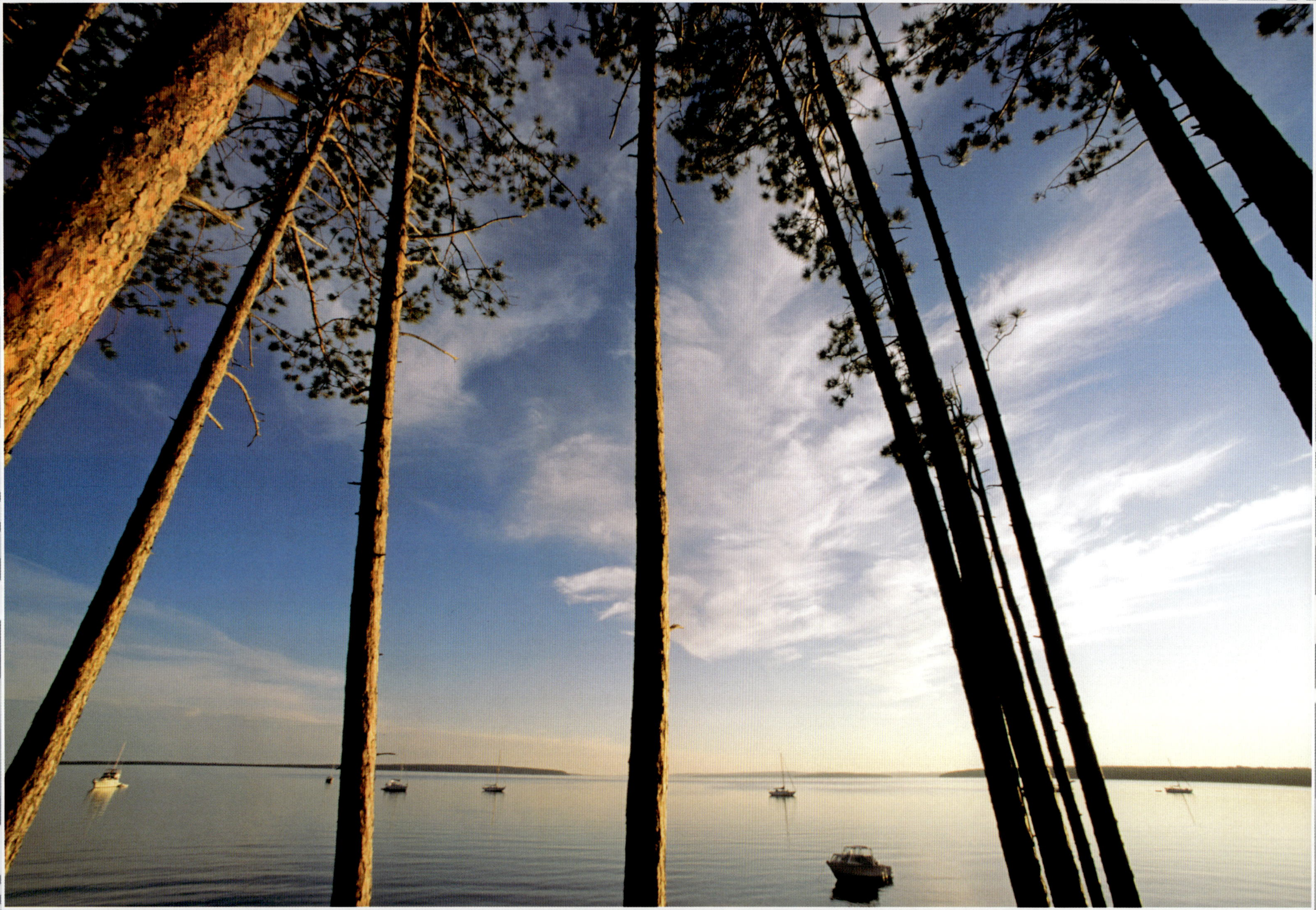

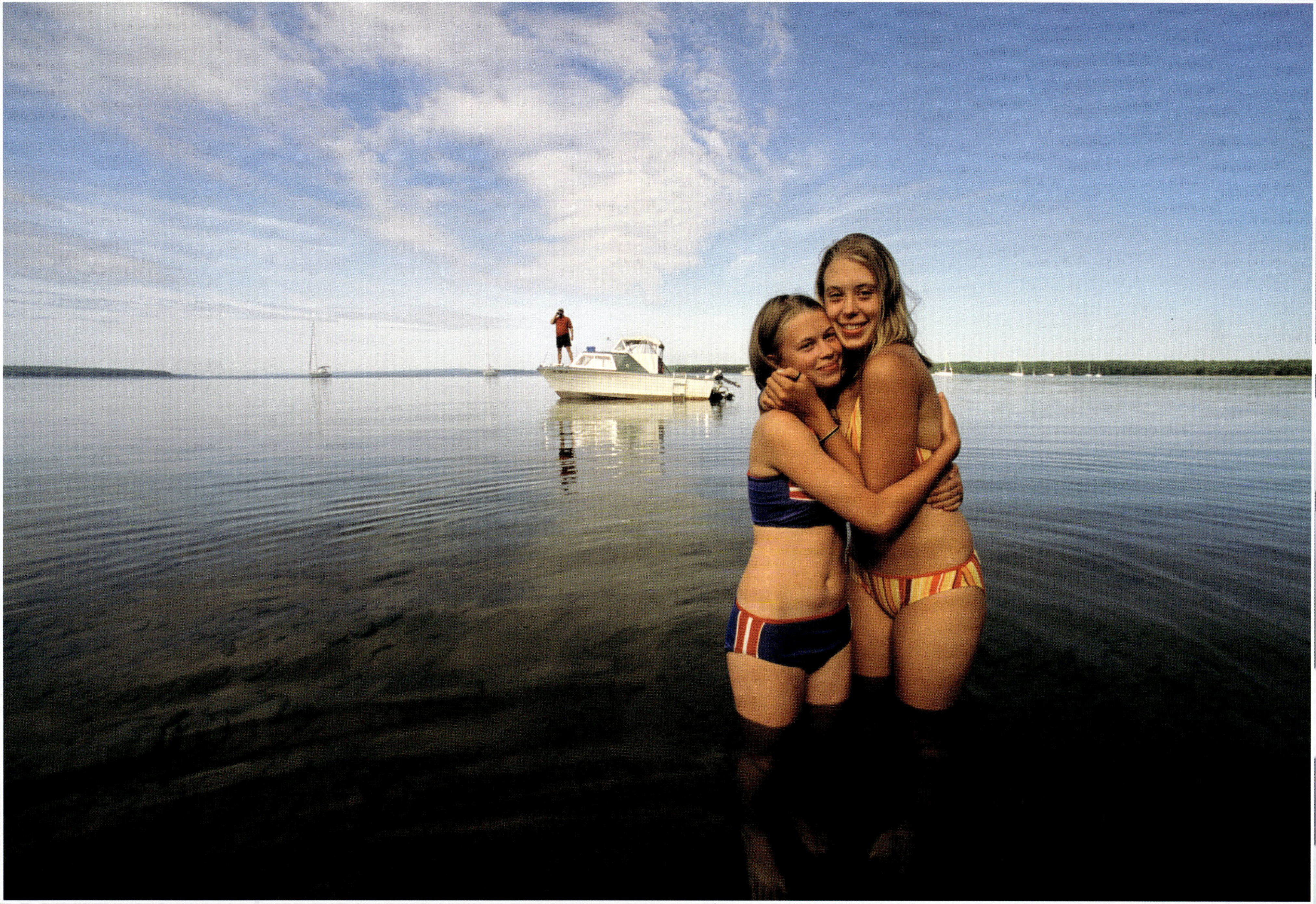

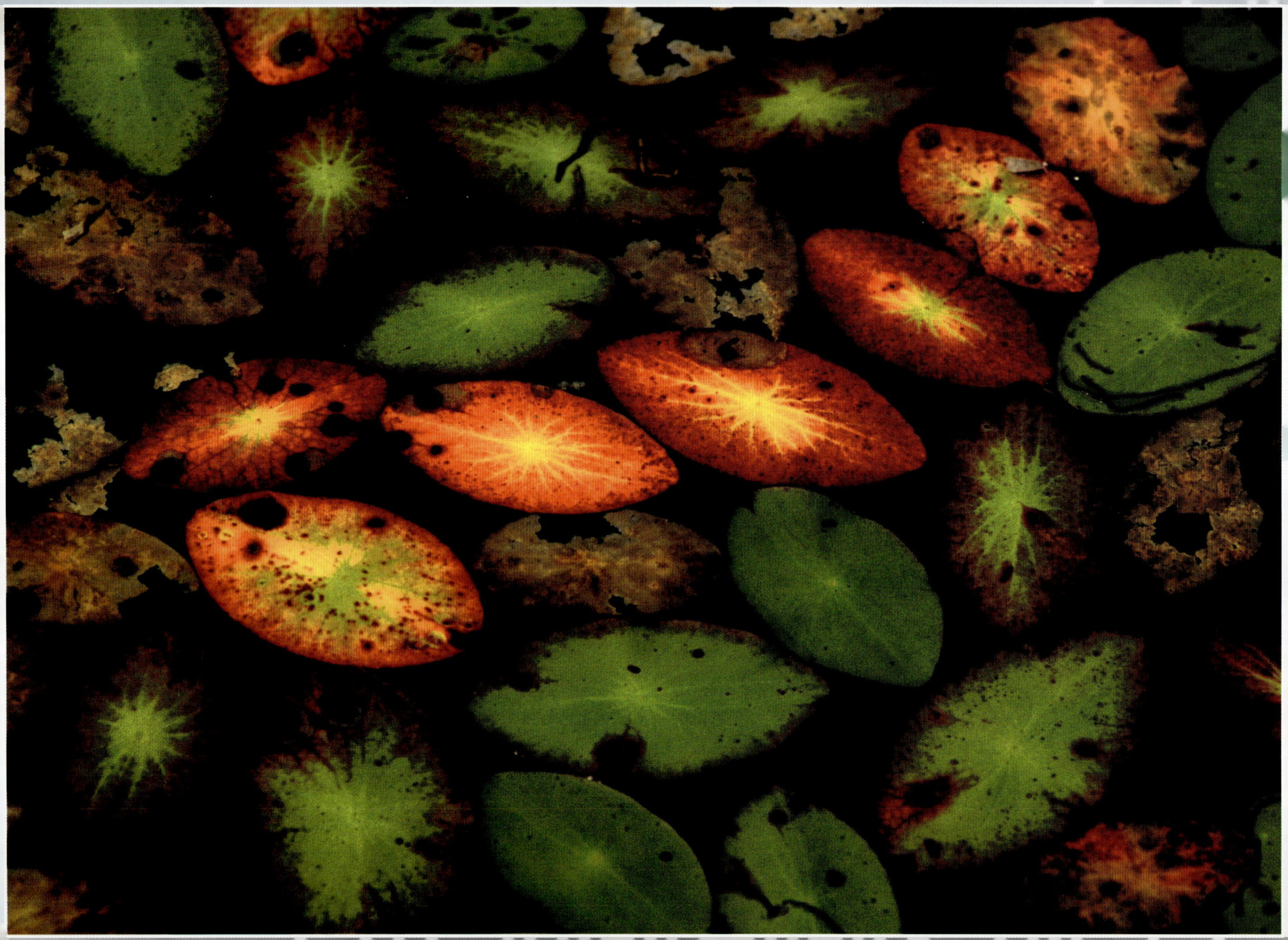

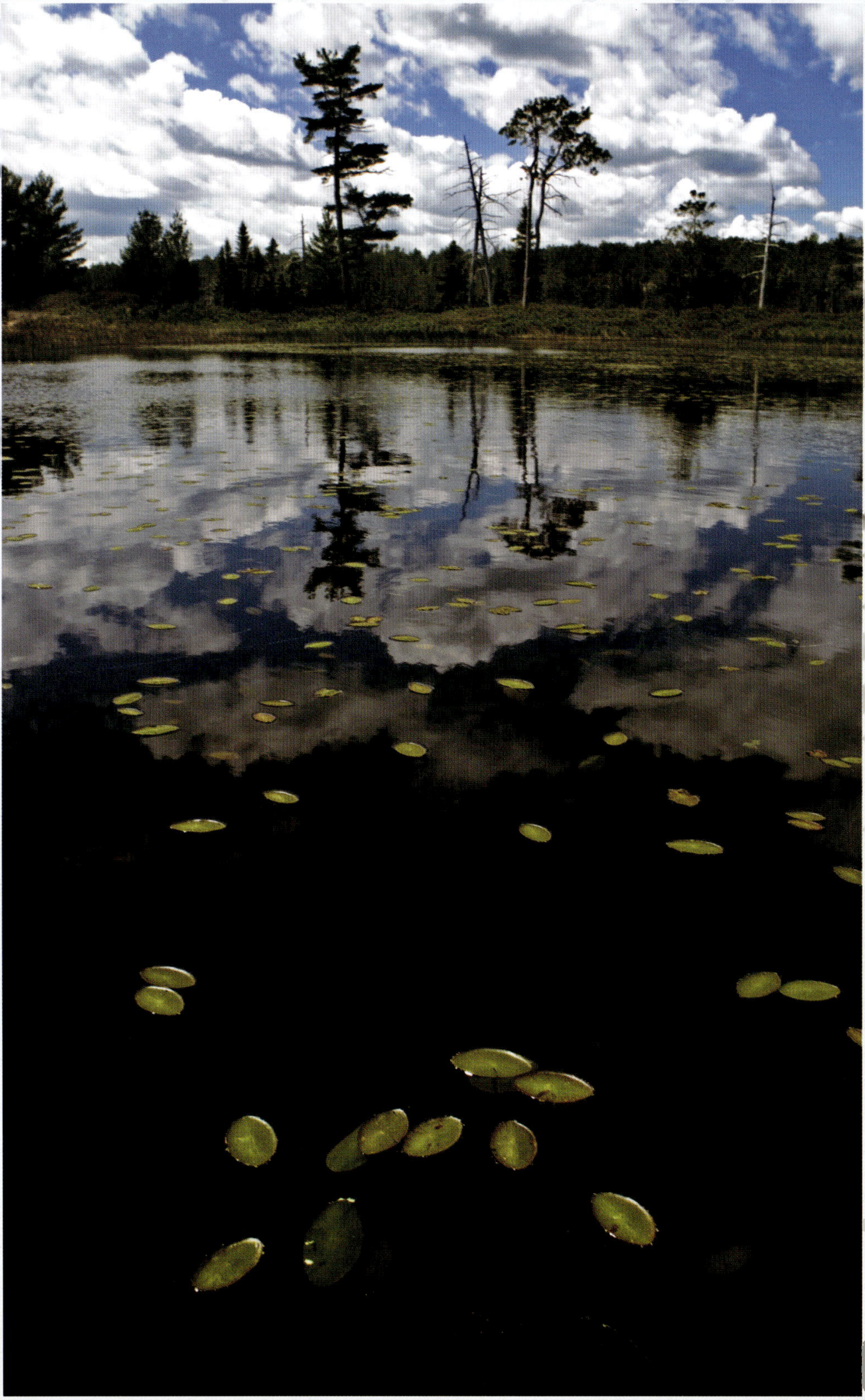

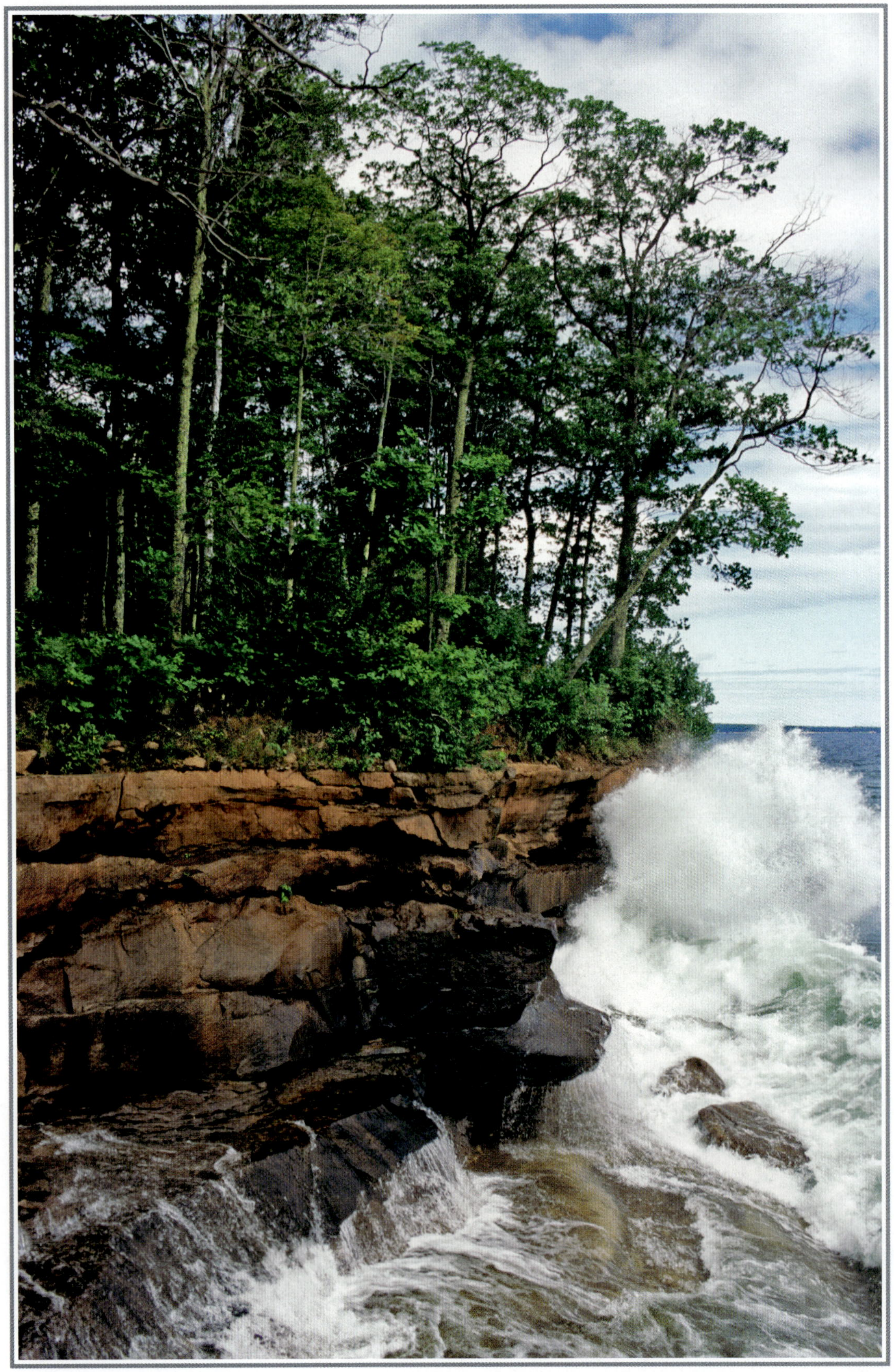

⚓ 115

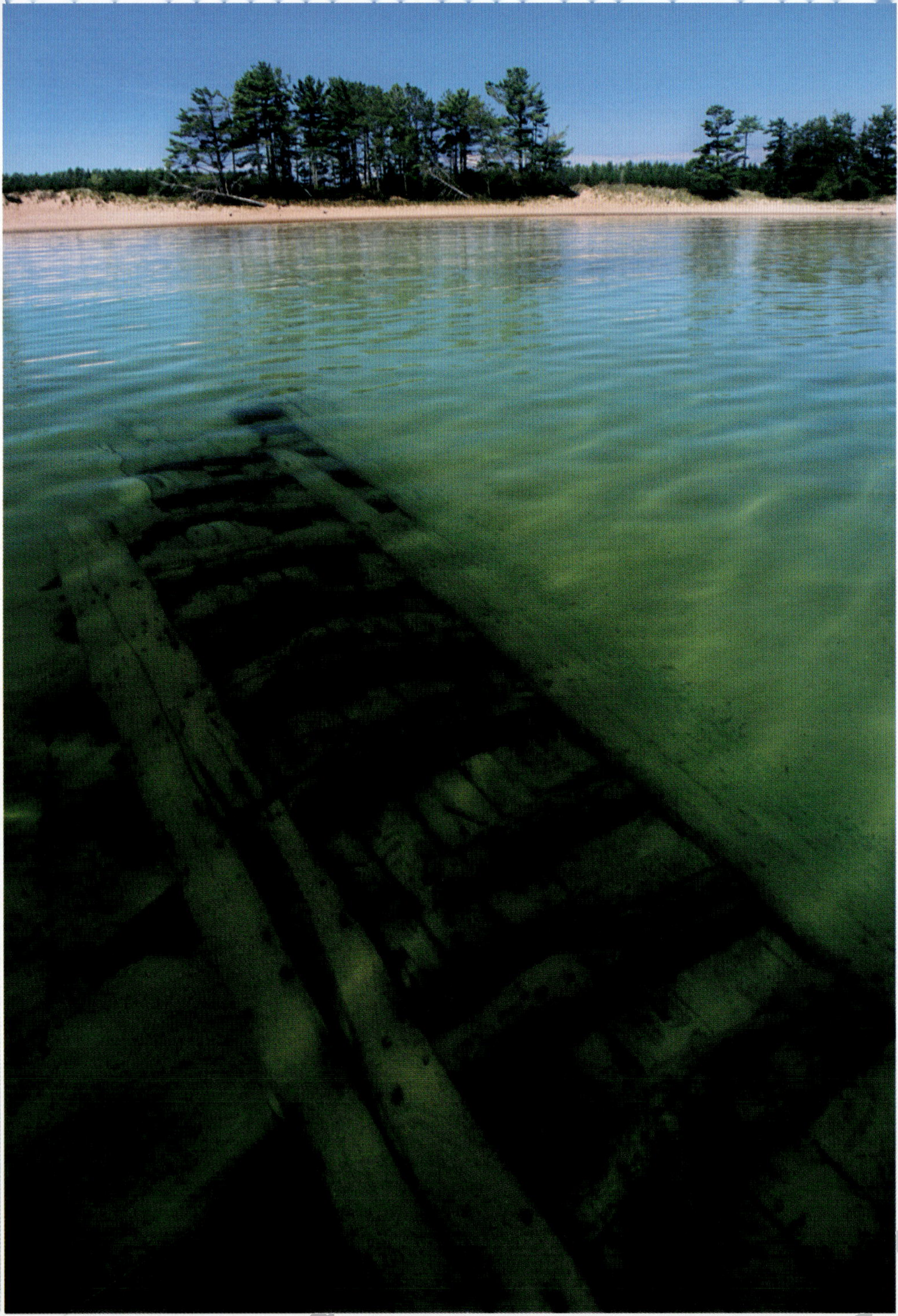

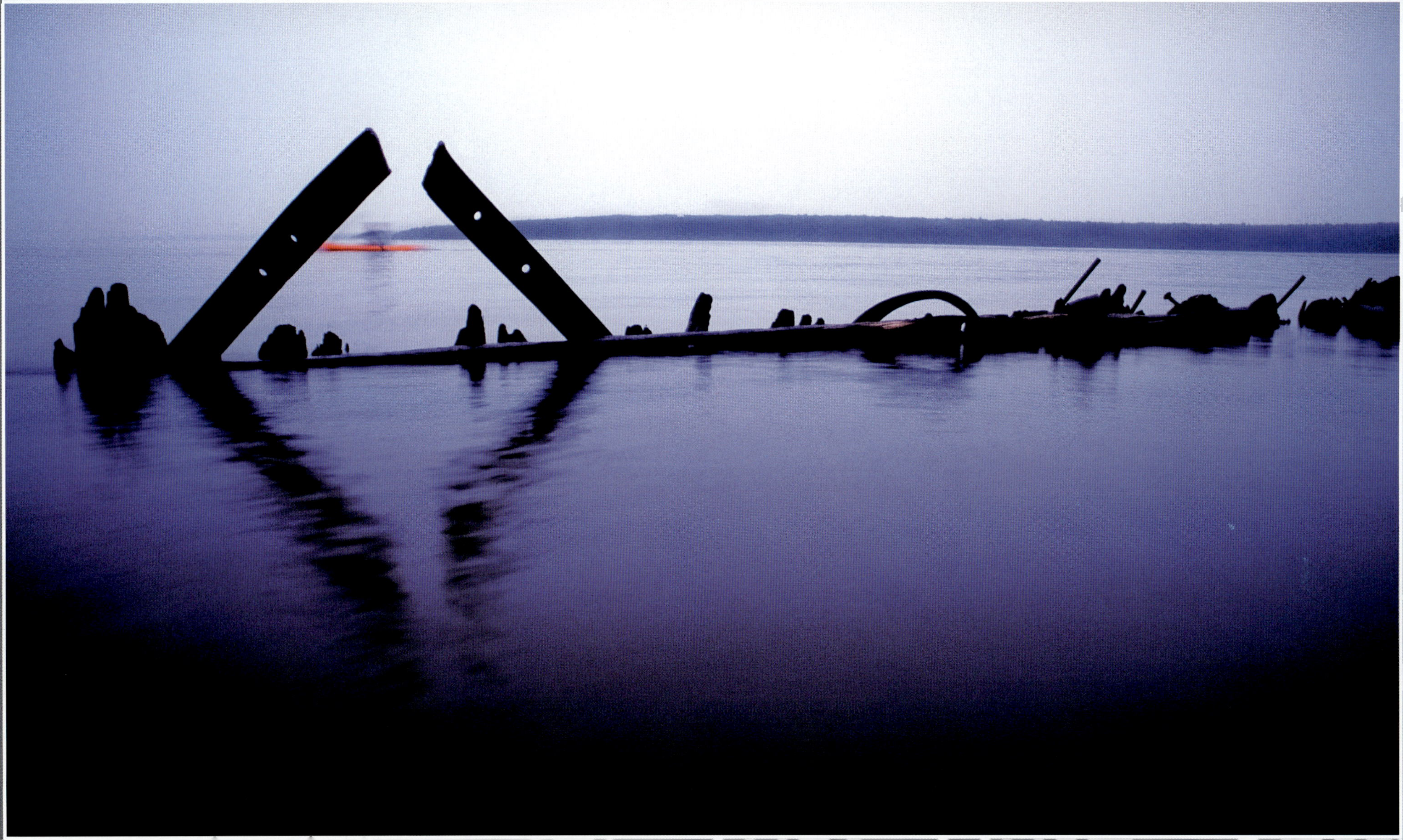

118

⚓ 119

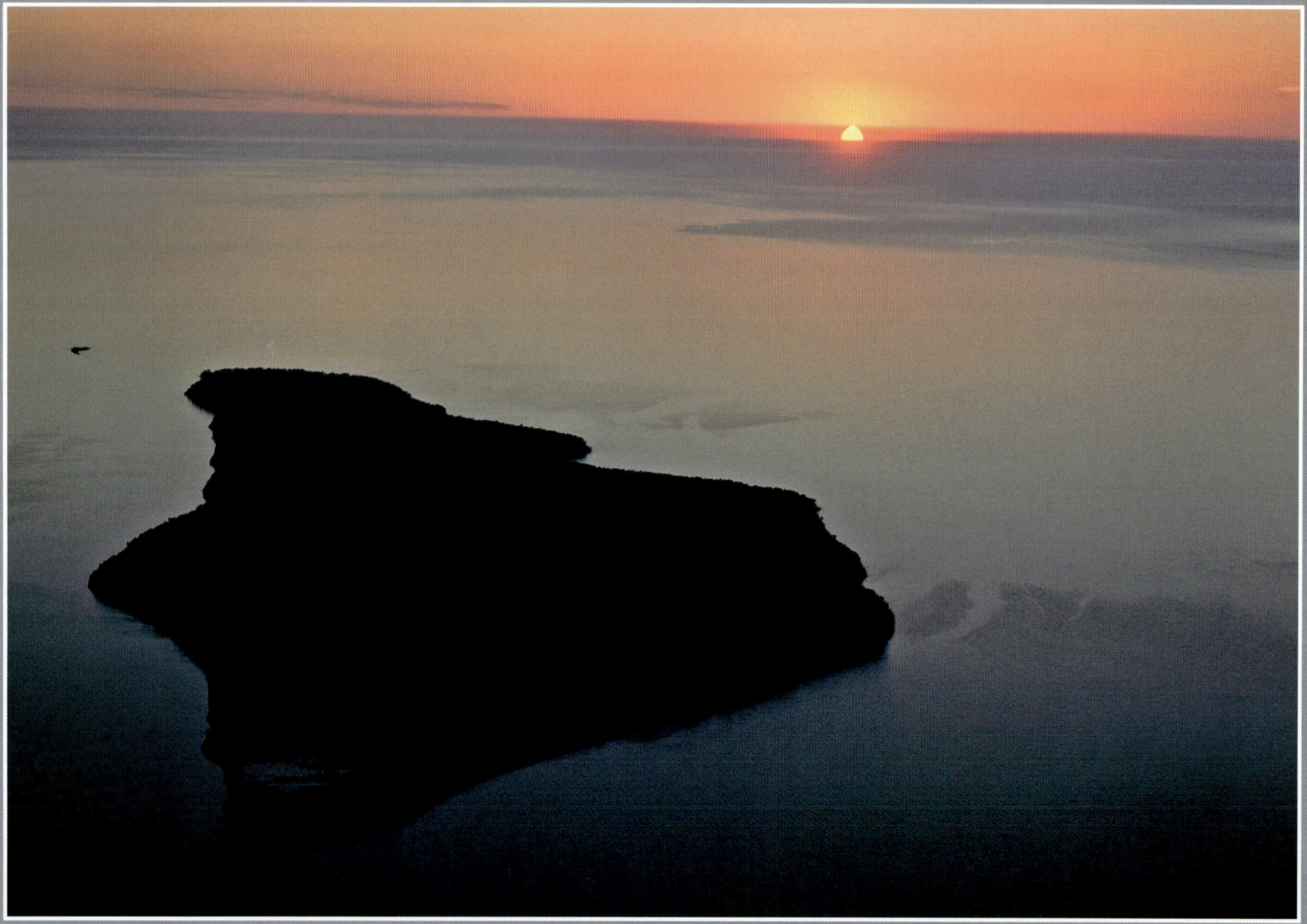

⚓ *121*

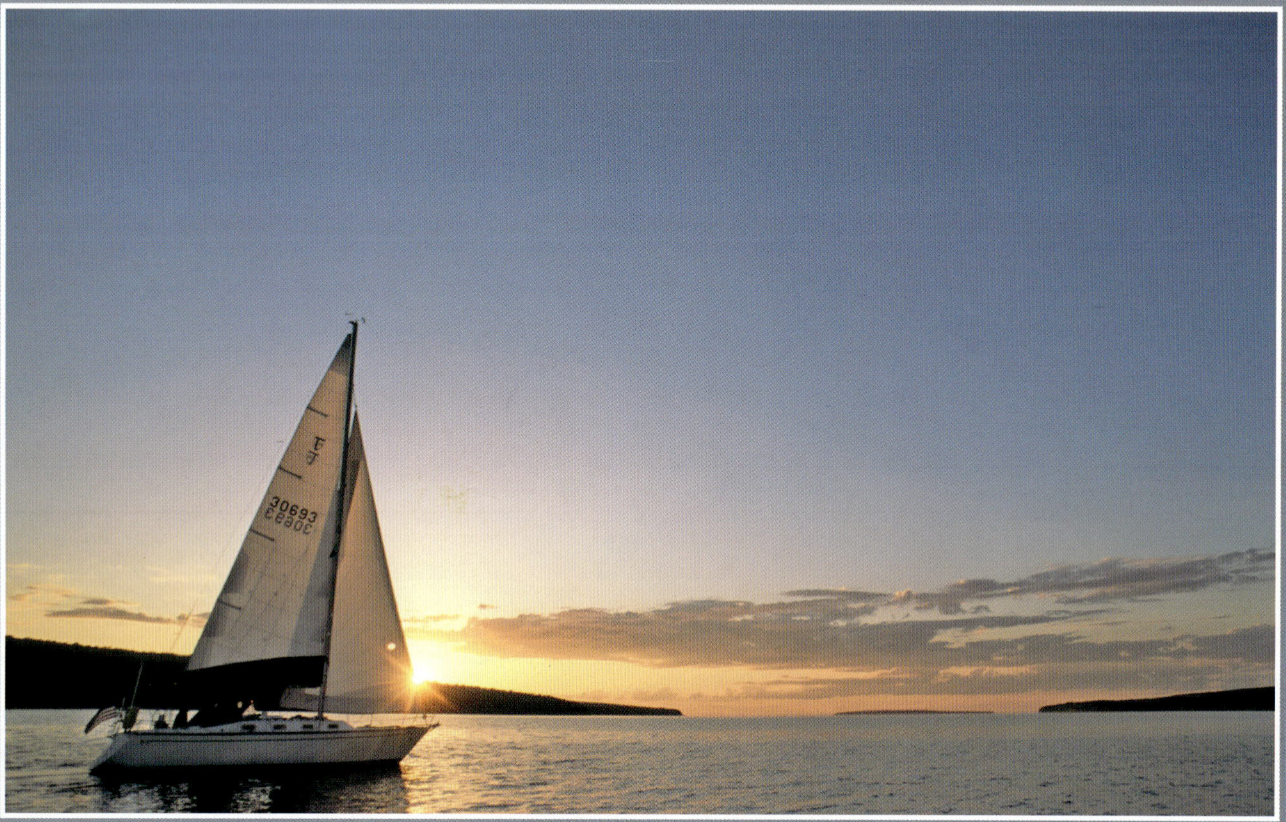
30693

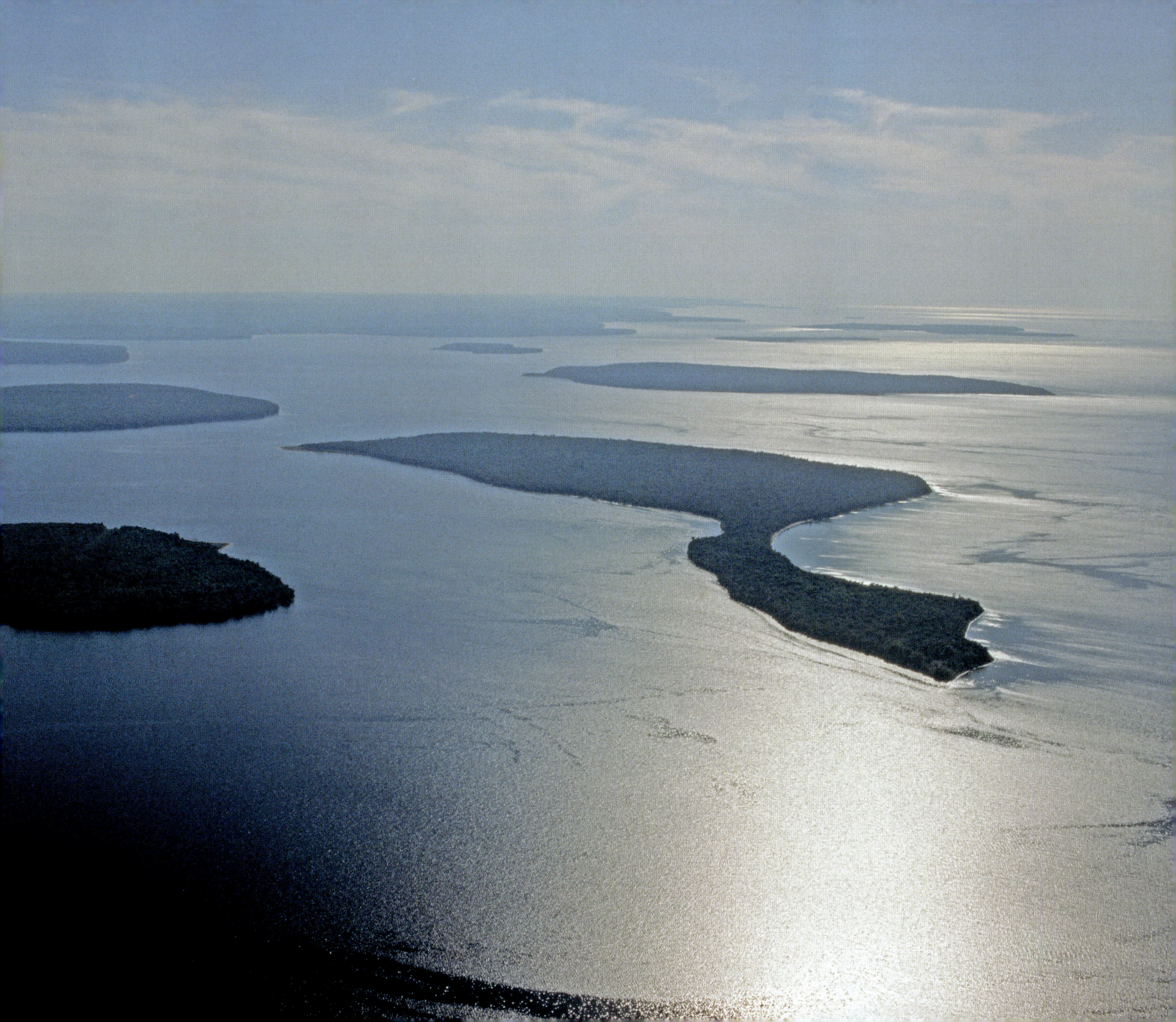

124

⚓ 125

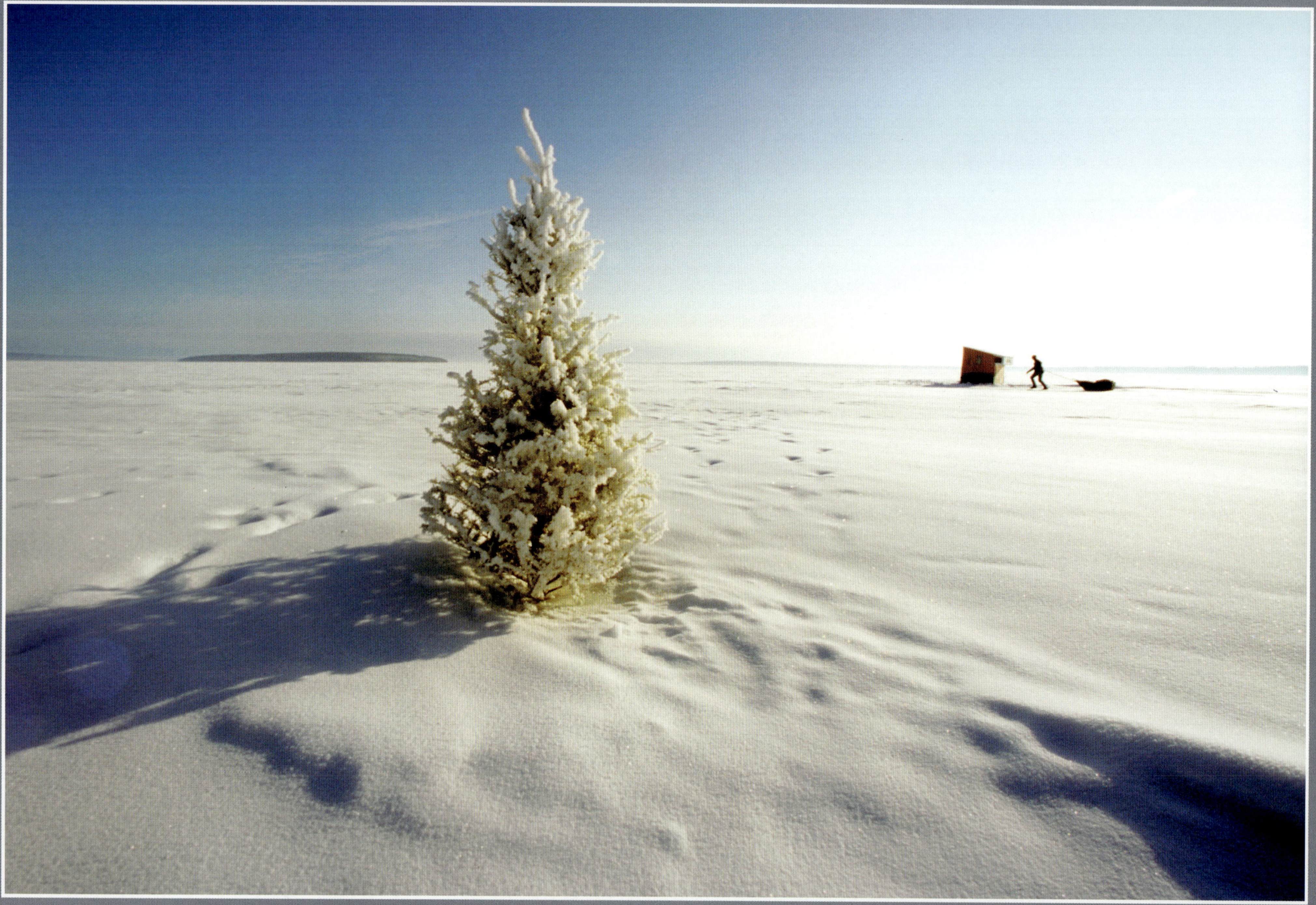

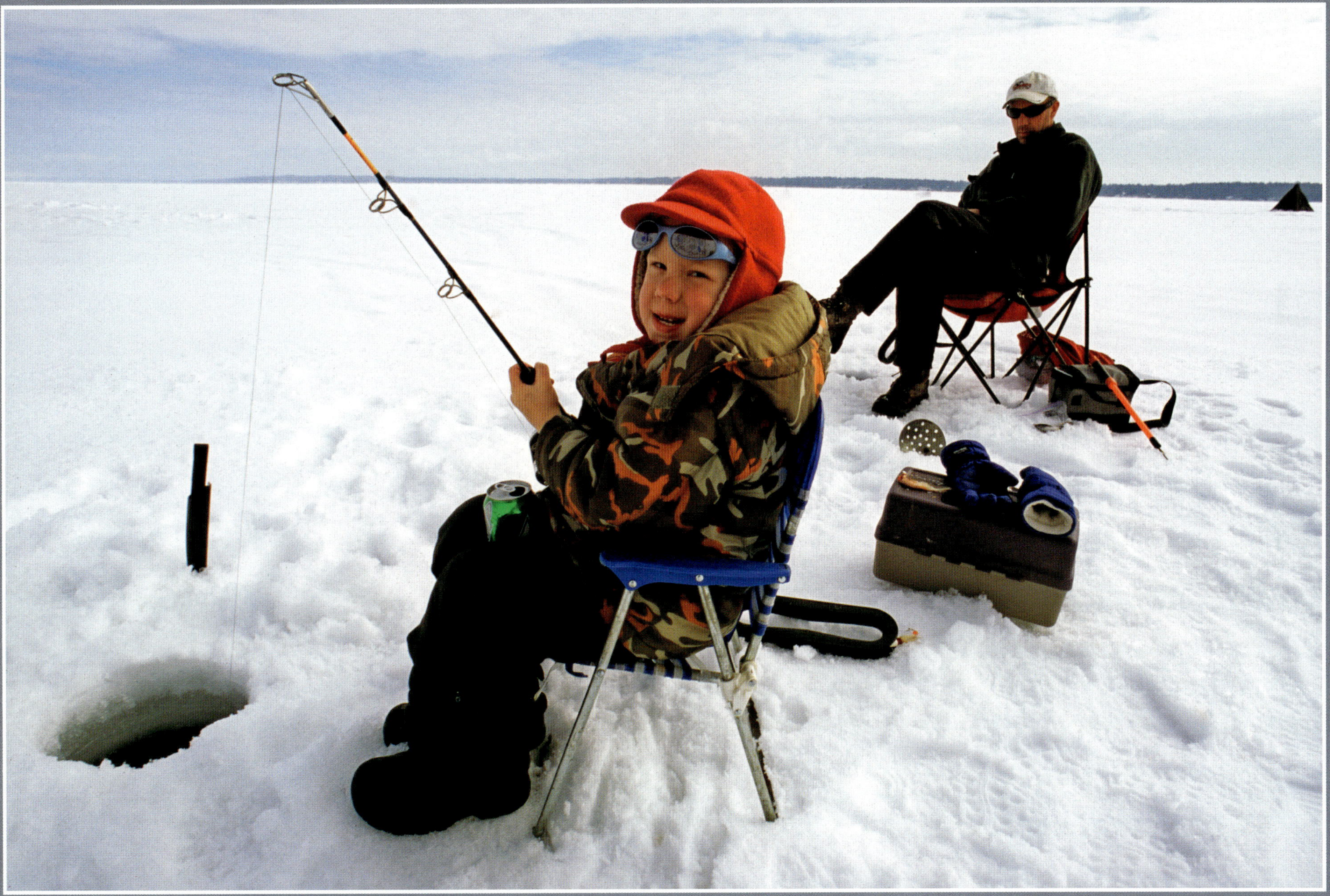

Location and subject notes for uncaptioned photographs:

Page 1. Sunset seen from Outer Island looking toward Cat and North Twin Islands
Page 2. Aerial view over Bayfield looking toward Basswood Island
Page 3. Aerial view of Outer Island
Pages 4-5. Sand Island sea caves
Page 8. Circle Islands sailboat race
Page 9. Sailboat seen from the sea caves on Sand Island
Page 10. Kayaker exploring the cliffs and caves on Sand Island
Page 11. Kayakers setting up camp on York Island
Page 98. A yellow warbler on Outer Island
Page 99. Fall color on Hermit Island
Page 100. Aerial view of an island ledge
Page 101. Stockton Island shelf fungus; spring foliage on Bear Island; white pine on Hermit Island; lupine on Outer Island
Page 102. Swimmer at York Island
Page 103. Sandstone shelves on Devils Island
Page 104. Faithful, an abandoned tug on Outer Island
Page 105. Outer Island sandspit with Stockton Island in the distance
Page 106. Oak Island sandspit
Page 107. Honeymoon Rock off Basswood Island
Page 108. Cooking fresh lake trout on Outer Island; starry night and campsite on Sand Island; sailboat anchored for the night near South Twin Island
Page 109. Waders at York Island beach
Page 110. Stockton Island's Presque Isle Bay campground looking south
Page 111. Two sisters hugging each other for warmth in Presque Isle Bay
Page 112. Lily pads on Stockton Island
Page 113. Stockton Island bog
Page 114. Crashing waves on Madeline Island
Page 115. Wave action on sandstone along the mainland shore
Page 116. Wreck of the ship Noque Bay in Julian Bay
Page 117. Wreck of the ship Fedora and a kayaker paddling nearby
Page 118. Tanin-stained waters that feed into Lake Superior from Sand Island
Page 119. Old car on Sand Island; fall leaves on a pond at Basswood quarry site
Page 120. Aerial view of Michigan Island at sunrise
Page 121. Storm seen from Hermit Island looking toward Madeline Island
Page 122. Sailboat headed west on Lake Superior
Page 123. Aerial view of the islands
Page 124. Storm over the lake
Page 125. Fog on Basswood Island
Page 126. An ice fisherman heading to his shack and one of many Christmas trees placed to mark the temporary ice road between Bayfield and Madeline Island
Page 127. A young boy and his father ice-fishing in the bay near Bayfield
Page 128 (above). The vastness of Lake Superior becomes evident as a clearing storm brings a dogsled musher from near white-out conditions to one with views of the distant islands. Travel over the ice of Superior can be chancy, due to shifting ice and changing visibility.

128